Beginner's Guide to Growing Wealth and Investing Copy

Planting Seeds & Growing Riches

Dr. Stacker

STACKERS UNIVERSITY

Stackers University

Published by Stackers University Press
Imprint of Stackers University, LLC

ISBN: 979-8-9931439-0-3

First Edition, 2025

Disclaimer
Stackers University is a brand name and is neither a chartered university nor an accredited educational institution. This book is provided for educational and informational purposes only and does not constitute financial, legal, tax, or investment advice.

The author and publisher make no representations or warranties regarding the accuracy or completeness of the contents, and they shall not be held liable for any loss, damages, or results incurred as a result of applying the information in this book.

As an investor, you are more important than any single investment instrument. Each reader must make their own decisions, accept responsibility for their outcomes, and verify information independently. Readers are strongly encouraged to consult with

licensed professionals for advice tailored to their individual circumstances.

Trademark Notice
Stackers Wealth Cycle™, Breaking the Working Poor Cycle, and *Working Poor Cycle™* are trademarks of Stackers University, LLC.

Contact
For information, permissions, or bulk orders, please visit:
http://www.stackersuniversity.com
Or email us at: contact@stackersuniversity.com

Contents

WELCOME TO STACKERS UNIVERSITY   VI

    The Stackers University Challenge

    How to Use This Guide: Your Roadmap to Wealth

    How to Navigate this Guide

    Lead Like A CIO, Grow Like A Gardener

THE GARDEN OF WOE   XIV

STAGE 1

   1. Introduction: Preparing the Soil   2

   2. Step Into The Role   4

   3. Why Being Broke Isn't Your Fault   6

   4. The Money Monkey Trap   9

   5. Should You Invest While In Debt?   12

   6. The Lies You Were Sold About Wealth   16

   7. Every Dollar Is An Employee...   20

   8. Now Hiring: Chief Investment Officer (CIO) of You, Inc.   22

   9. You're Hired   24

  10. Tools   26

STAGE 2

  11. Introduction: Planting the Seeds   32

  12. What Is Investing (Really)?   34

13. Time Is Your Superpower   36

14. Inflation: The Silent Thief   39

15. The Investor's Toolbox   41

16. Understanding Investment Costs, Fees & Expense Ratios   50

17. Tax-Advantaged Accounts: Your Secret Weapon   53

18. Risk vs. Reward: What Every Smart CIO Understands   54

19. Understanding Return on Investment (ROI)   57

20. Tools   60

21. Risk Tolerance Quiz   64

STAGE 3

22. Introduction: Designing the Garden   68

23. Build The Infrastructure   69

24. Money Flow = Water For The Garden   71

25. Paying Yourself First   75

26. Automate Your Wealth Cycle   78

27. The Planting Guide   81

28. Tools   86

29. Step-by-Step Trade Practice Guide   90

STAGE 4

30. Introduction: Weathering the Seasons   94

31. "Weather"-Proof Your Mindset   95

32. Outsmarting Your Emotions   97

33. Tools   100

STAGE 5

34. Introduction: The Fruit-Bearing Tree   106

35. Scaling With Intention   107

36. Generational Wealth Starts With You   109

37. Creating Your Wealth Cycle   111

38. Putting It Into Motion   121

39. Tools   123

NEXT MOVES

40. You're Different Now!   128

41. Tools   131

APPENDICES

42. Appendix A: Glossary of Terms   136

43. Appendix B: Summary of Core ETFs   140

44. Appendix C: Nota Bene   143

DEDICATION   148

ABOUT THE AUTHOR   150

45. YOUR NOTA BENE NOTES   152

WELCOME TO STACKERS UNIVERSITY

It's not about being an investor, it's about being the type of person that can invest.

Welcome to the *Beginner's Guide to Investing and Growing Wealth: Planting Seeds & Growing Riches.* This isn't just about money, it's about rewriting the story of how you live, lead, and build what lasts. Whether you've never owned a single stock or you've dabbled here and there without a clear strategy, this guide was created for one reason: to put you in control, not just of your money, but of your mindset, your confidence, and your future. Let's be real. Most of us didn't grow up talking about investing at the dinner table. We weren't taught how to think about risk, retirement, or building wealth over time. For many of us, money was either a source of stress, something we didn't discuss, or both. **That ends here!**

Inside this guide, you're going to do more than just learn how investing works; you're going to step into your new role. From this moment forward, you're the Chief Investment Officer (CIO) of You, Inc. That means you make the calls. You direct your dollars. You grow what you've been given. This isn't about chasing get-rich-quick schemes. This is about building get-rich-for-sure habits – intentionally and strategically. Like planting a fruit tree, the results aren't instant, but they are inevitable when you follow the process. And to grow those riches? You need to lead like a gardener and think like a CEO. You're not just here to learn how investing works; you're here to lead your financial life differently.

To think differently.
To grow differently.

Before we grow wealth, we need to prepare the soil. This guide doesn't just show you how to invest, it teaches you how to grow wealth from the ground up.

Starting with mindset. Reinforced by habits. Anchored in systems that support your goals.

By the time you finish, you'll have the knowledge to start and the mindset to stick with it. Wealth-building isn't about picking the right investments; it's about picking yourself and backing that decision with action. This book is for:

- Those tired of confusion, fear, and financial shame.

- Those seeking clarity, security, and a practical plan.

- Those who want to build something solid and lasting, not just flashy.

People like us.

Plant Today. Prosper Tomorrow. Wealth is not built by luck. It's built by intention. This guide will show you how to start planting the right seeds today, so your future self can eat the fruit of those decisions tomorrow. *Let's plant something powerful.*

— Dr. Stacker

The Stackers University Challenge

Don't just read this guidebook... Live it.

This isn't just another book; it's your launchpad. Now it's time to move from learning to leading to getting real-world wins. Here's your challenge:

1. Build your wealth cycle using the tools in this guide.

2. Commit to one action this week, even if it's small.

3. Pick one person to share what you've learned.

4. Join the Stackers community, share your progress, and be the inspiration someone else needs.

5. Revisit this book in 6 months and see how far you've come.

As motivational speaker Les Brown said, "It's the start that stops most people." So just start! Forget perfect. Forget waiting. The biggest mistake is not beginning. Wealth isn't built in theory; it's built in motion.

> Movement builds momentum. Momentum builds pressure, power, and presence. It makes you harder to stop... And harder for you to quit.

You're ready to start planting, building, and growing. And now that you're in motion, you're a problem for anything trying to hold you back, especially the old version of you. You're on a mission now, and the version of you that settles won't make it past this point.

How to Use This Guide: Your Roadmap to Wealth

This isn't just a book. It's a transformation plan.

You're not here to memorize terms or follow hype; this is about you becoming the kind of person who can invest consistently, confidently, and in alignment with your future. This guide is designed to walk you step-by-step through the mindset, tools, and systems required to lead your financial life like a Chief Investment Officer (CIO) and grow your money like a gardener. Whether you're starting with $5 or $5,000, the process is the same: build from the ground up, and let time and intention do the heavy lifting.

How to Navigate this Guide

1. Move Stage-by-Stage — Don't Rush the Roots

The guide is divided into five transformational stages, each one building on the last:

- You'll start with mindset (preparing the soil).

- Then plant the seeds of time and compounding.

- Then design your Wealth Cycle system.

- Then weather the seasons with discipline.

- And finally, harvest freedom and legacy as your Wealth Cycle bears fruit.

By the end of this journey, you won't just understand investing, you'll step fully into your new identity as a confident investor. This book isn't about skimming for hot tips or reading this like a textbook; you're building a wealth operating system, one decision at a time.

2. Use the Tools — Don't Skip the Practice

This guide is filled with worksheets, checklists, cheat sheets, and reflection prompts to help you internalize the lessons. These are not "extras," they're essential. If information is the seed, action is the water. Look for:

- CIO Insights – mindset shifts that shape behavior

- Reflection Prompts – turn lessons into clarity

- Printable Tools – plug-and-play assets you can use now

- Examples and Scenarios – to make every concept real

3. Reflect Often — Your Growth Is the Real ROI (Return On Investment)

Each section of this guide was intentionally structured to mirror the growth journey of a long-term investor, helping you move from someone unsure where to start to someone confidently planting seeds for long-term wealth. It is truly a journey and reflecting allows you to find deeper connections with and meaning from this experience.

4. Return to This Guide Again and Again

This isn't a "one and done" read. Come back to this as your income grows, your goals shift, and your system evolves. Revisit the tools. Track your progress. Upgrade your strategy.

5. Trust the Process — You're Becoming a CIO

Don't worry if it doesn't all click at once. Stick with the system. Ask questions. Make mistakes. The goal isn't perfection. It's progress, consistency, and confidence.

Remember This: Before you grow your wealth, you have to "grow yourself." Let this guide be your coach, your accountability partner, and your blueprint for financial leadership. Let's get started. The garden awaits.

Lead Like A CIO, Grow Like A Gardener

Understanding the Metaphors: CIO & Planting

This guide uses two powerful metaphors to help you understand, apply, and remember the lessons inside. They work together, not against each other, to build both your mindset and your methods.

The CIO Metaphor = Role + Responsibility

Throughout this book, you'll hear the phrase "CIO of You, Inc." That's not just clever branding; it's about a mindset shift that needs to happen. You are the Chief Investment Officer of your financial life. That means:

- You are the strategist, not a spectator.

- You're responsible for deploying your dollars like a manager assigns employees.

- You evaluate opportunities, manage risks, and build long-term systems.

Why This Mindset Works

Calling yourself the CIO isn't just about having a title. It's about stepping into an identity, one that demands clarity, structure, and purpose. Most people drift through life hoping their money will somehow work itself out. But hope isn't a strategy. As CIO, you stop hoping and start building. You stop reacting to your finances and start leading them using a system aligned with your vision. You don't need to know everything on day one; you just need to show up like it matters, because it does. The power behind this new identity is critical, because investing:

> Isn't just about money… It's about becoming someone new… It's about becoming an investor… A builder… A leader of wealth, not just a chaser of dollars.

When you treat this role like your life mission, you'll show up differently. You'll build systems and start thinking long-term because your financial life will have your attention. Your attention will allow you to develop a strong intention, because attention energizes, and intention transforms. This guide will help you rewire the way you see money and yourself.

The Planting Metaphor = Journey + Growth

While the CIO metaphor gives you a role, the planting metaphor gives you a story.

> Every dollar is a seed…Every financial habit is watering the soil…Every investment is a step toward harvest.

This metaphor reminds you that real wealth is organic, not instant. Like planting a tree, you don't see results immediately, but with time, care and patience, your efforts will yield exponential growth. This guidebook follows that rhythm:

- Stage 1: Preparing the Soil

- Stage 2: Planting the Seeds

- Stage 3: Designing the Garden

- Stage 4: Weathering the Seasons

- Stage 5: The Fruit-Bearing Tree

- Next Season, Next Moves: You're Not A Beginner Anymore

You are both the architect and the gardener: leading with vision, building with systems, and nurturing your wealth to life.

Flip the Script on Wealth
As crazy as it sounds, one of the biggest barriers to wealth isn't money, it's mindset. If you believe wealth is only for the elite, people with six-figure incomes, or those that get lucky, then your actions will match that belief. You won't believe, you'll find excuses, you'll blame others, you won't find success because you'll believe the barriers were external to you and out of your control. That kind of thinking is a thief, a thief that steals your motivation, your action, and your potential. But here's the truth:

> You don't have to know everything in order to start. But you do have to start.

Les Brown said it best: "It's the start that stops most people." So let this be your start by stepping into this role. Start with belief, and even if you don't believe, start with action until belief shows up. You just might surprise yourself.

Reflection Prompt: Step Into the Role
You are now the Chief Investment Officer of You, Inc. That title means something. It comes with weight, purpose, ownership, and responsibility. Take a few minutes to reflect on what that means for you personally.

Prompt:

- What beliefs or behaviors do you need to leave behind to step fully into this role?

- What kind of leader do you want to be for your money?

- What would the future version of you, the financially secure one, thank you for doing today?

Belief Tracker: Rewrite the Script
Wealth-building isn't just about what you do; it's about what you believe. In this exercise, we'll surface the beliefs you might be carrying and give you space to replace them with something stronger. Fill in the right side of the table below with new beliefs that support your identity as the CIO of You, Inc. You don't have to believe them 100% yet — just start practicing the mindset you're growing into.

Old Belief (Taught/Learned/Assumed)	New Belief (Taught/Learned/Assumed)
I'm not good with money.	
I'm too late to start.	
Investing is only for rich people.	
I'll never understand this stuff.	
If I make a mistake, I'll lose everything.	
I need to wait until I have more money.	
Money is confusing and stressful.	

Pro Tip: Beliefs Aren't Fixed. They're Planted.
Some grow strong and shape your future, while others become weeds. When a belief stops serving you, don't water it; uproot it, and plant a new one. The new beliefs you're writing down...They're seeds. You won't believe them fully at first and that's okay. But like any planted seed, they grow through repetition, action, and nurturing. Don't wait to feel confident. Move like someone who's building confidence and let your belief catch up.

THE GARDEN OF WOE

You can't grow wealth in the soil of regret, but you can start planting something new.

L et me tell you about a place every investor visits at least once - a place I call *The Garden of Woe.*

It's that plot of land where rue, regret and remorse thrive.
Where the soil lies between what you knew and what you did.
Old fears, doubts, and missed chances grow side by side.
While weeds named: Wish-I-Had, One-Day and Should-Have run wild.

It's a garden rich with fertilizer made of excuses.
Watered by tears and fears.
Sunned by the relentless heat of regret.
The ground resists new dreams;
Vines of "*What If*" twist around every half-planted goal.

Birds sing sad songs of what could have been.
Here, what's possible feels unrealistic.
Visions of a new beginning feel overwhelming.
The Garden of Woe becomes where you watch your mistakes flourish.

The Garden of Woe is not beyond repair.
That same soil still has power.
The Garden of Woe isn't cursed ground.
It's just untended ground waiting for your hands.

You can pull up the weeds.
You can dig again.
You can replant right here, right now.
You can nurture what you want to flourish.

Every dollar you save is a seed.
Every deposit you make is a starter plant.
Every investment made is fertilizer for your soil.
Every time you choose discipline, you get closer to harvest.
And before long,
What used to be the Garden of Woe,
Becomes the Garden of *Whoa.*
A place where one day you say,
"Whoa... look what grew."
"Whoa... look at what I was able to do."

Stop staring at what died.
Stop staring at what you didn't want to grow.
Stop waiting for perfect weather.

Pick up your tools.
Pull your fear up by the root.
Start planting again.

The harvest is still waiting on you.
The Garden of Woe needs you.
The Garden of Whoa -
Your Garden of Wealth -
Needs your attention.

The Garden of Woe isn't just a story, it's a reflection of what most of us do. Every one of us has stood in that soil, looking down at what didn't grow. We've all said, *"If only I had started sooner." "If only I had saved more." "If only I had spent smarter."* None of those sentences water your future, they only feed the weeds.

Regret isn't punishment; it's valuable information, the heart's way of saying, *"I care about what could have been."* But once it's done its job of getting your attention, its purpose ends. Forgive yourself for what you didn't know or what you didn't do. If you were capable of doing better back then, you would have. Now is the time to get back to the soil, back to the garden. Every limiting belief you uproot, every new seed you plant, is you rewriting the story of yesterday. The goal isn't to erase your past; it's to outgrow it. And the only way to redeem lost time is to *plant now.*

Forgive yourself. Forgive the old you. Release the timeline you thought you should be on. Everyone looks back and sees missed chances. Ignore how everyone else's garden is growing. President Theodore Roosevelt said it best: *"Comparison is the thief of joy.*" The difference between those who stay stuck and those who grow is this: Growers stop counting what's gone, stop comparing themselves to others, and start cultivating right where they are in life.

Look at your current garden (your finances, your habits, your mindset) and ask: What's still alive here? What can I replant right now? Because every new seed you drop into the ground moves you one day closer to fruit-bearing. Every act of discipline shortens the distance between who you were and who you're becoming. Soon enough, the same garden that once represented your regret will become the proof of your renewal, evidence that you didn't give up, you kept growing.

Reflection: Leaving the Garden of Woe
The Garden of Woe is a dangerous place to view your life from. Now is the time to leave that place behind so you can take what you've learned and start fresh. This is the bridge between who you were and who you're becoming. Before you move into Stage 1, *Planting the Seeds*, take a moment to prepare your inner soil. What you do from this point forward will shape everything that grows next.

Reflection Activity: From Woe to Grow
Use the space below to release regret and plant intention.

- **Pull the Weeds:** What regret, belief, or fear has been choking your growth? (Example: *"I waited too long." "I'll never catch up."*)

- **Amend the Soil:** What truth can you plant in its place, one that helps something better grow? (Example: *"It's not too late. Every seed planted now still compounds."*)

- **Choose Your First Seed:** What *small* action can you take this week to begin your new season of growth? *(Example: cut $20 from your weekly spending, save an extra $10, skip one unnecessary purchase, or move loose change into a "seed fund.")*

- **Commit to the Work:** Write one sentence that affirms your new direction. (Example: *"I'm done replaying what I didn't do and I am starting by growing with what I have."*)

Closing Note from Dr. Stacker
You can change how you show up from this point forward. What you just wrote are your first seeds, your first decisions in a new garden. Now, let's get our hands in the dirt.

Stage 1: Planting the Seeds begins now.

STAGE 1

PREPARING THE SOIL

Stackers University

Chapter One

Introduction: Preparing the Soil

Theme: Identity Shift: Break Ground & Old Beliefs
Goal: Let go of your consumer mindset, adopt your role as CIO, and prepare your foundation.

*B*efore anything can grow, the ground has to be broken. This stage is about clearing out the weeds: the old stories, beliefs, and habits that have been choking your financial growth. Maybe it's the belief that money is too complicated. Or that investing is only for the wealthy. Or that your past mistakes mean you can't build wealth. Not true.

This is where you reclaim your role, not as a passive consumer, but as the **Chief Investment Officer (CIO)** of your financial life. From this point forward, you don't just make money decisions, you lead them. Like a gardener prepping their plot, you're digging deep, pulling out roots that no longer serve you, and laying the groundwork for something better. *This is where your real wealth journey begins, with a mindset shift.*

If every dollar is an employee, then your money isn't just numbers on a screen, it's your workforce. Like any business, the question isn't how many employees you have, it's whether they're actually producing. A profitable business doesn't let people sit around collecting a paycheck, it makes sure every role is tied to results. The same goes for your dollars. Some will be builders; some will coast; some will slip away if you're not paying attention.

Your role as CIO is to lead a business where finances are managed with intention. Not just busy, not just moving, but productive, working in alignment with your vision and creating wealth on purpose.

Before you begin planting, you clear the soil. Before you invest, you lead your mindset. This is where the shift begins; no more passive consumption, no more drifting through financial decisions. From here forward, you're not just another person in the economy; you're a Chief Investment Officer running your own enterprise inside it. That's what this stage is really about. It's the root system, the foundation, the ground you plant into. You've broken the surface, you're digging in, pulling out the weeds, and loosening the soil that used to keep you stuck. Now the question becomes, how do you step into your role as the leader of this new enterprise?

The answer is found in identity. You are not just a spender, saver, or investor. You are the CIO of You, Inc., and like any effective leader, your next move is to define what that role really means and how you're going to carry it out.

Chapter Two

Step Into The Role

Let's go! This is where it all begins, not with a portfolio, a mountain of cash or a paycheck, but with a new perspective. You are the Chief Investment Officer (CIO) of You, Inc. It's a declaration that you must make to yourself. In this stage, you don't chase tactics; you challenge beliefs, begin breaking mental blocks, and start pulling the mental weeds so you can make room for what you're growing.

Because you don't build wealth by accident; it's built on purpose with patience, with diligence, with systems, and with identity. Let's get your hands in the soil.

Welcome to the Role of CIO
As the CIO, you're no longer a bystander in your financial life which means you have to understand some hard truths.

Truth #1: Money Doesn't Make You Wealthy
Wealth isn't just about how much money you have; it's about how well that money works for you. Income is important, but without systems, purpose, and intention, it disappears. This is why wealth is measured in freedom, not figures.

Truth #2: Investing Isn't Just for the Rich
Dismiss the often-repeated lie that you need to be wealthy to invest. The truth is you become wealthy by investing. Throughout the guide we will break down the myths that keep people stuck and show you how everyday people build extraordinary futures: one decision at a time.

Truth #3: Building Wealth Is a System, Not a Secret
Wealthy people aren't lucky; they're structured and use automation to build repeatable systems that generate returns over time.

Belief Flips That Make You Rich

Your mindset is your greatest asset or your biggest liability. We will continually highlight the limiting beliefs that hold people back and replace them with empowering truths that align with your new role as CIO. The rich and wealthy know that:

- Dollars are employees and you must make them work

- The primary purpose of money is not to pay bills

A critical concept to understand is that your dollars are not for everyone else; they are your employees. Every dollar you spend or save either becomes a worker for your business or someone else's. The more your dollars are tied up in bills, rent, or random spending, the fewer you have working for you. If you hand your money over to Amazon, it goes to work for Bezos. Swipe it at Target? That dollar's now building someone else's empire. But when you trim unneeded spending, save and invest it intentionally, your dollars "clock" in for your business, for your future. The rich and wealthy don't see money as something to spend; they see it as a workforce, and every dollar has a job to do. So, the questions then become:

- How many of your employees do you keep every month?

- Is your workforce expanding or shrinking?

- Are they building something for you?

Make the commitment: Going forward, you're not just surviving, you're building. Let's grow.

Chapter Three

Why Being Broke Isn't Your Fault

... But It's Still Your Responsibility

S omething needs to be said before you go any further: *If you've been broke, struggling, or confused about money, it's not your fault.* You were never supposed to win the financial game, because the system isn't designed to help you win. Almost literally, the system wants you to be broke and overspending. As W. Edwards Deming said:

> *"Every system is perfectly designed to get the results it gets."*

And our financial system? It's designed to keep most people broke.

A System That Trains You To Spend

From the moment you enter school, you're conditioned to be a good employee, not a good business owner or investor. You're taught to follow instructions, trade your time for money, and avoid risk. You're never taught how to build wealth. You're never taught how to use money as a tool. You're never taught to think like a builder of wealth. Then as you get older, and it only gets worse. Everywhere you turn, you're bombarded with messages designed to have you:

- Consume More

- Spend more

- Upgrade this or that

- Finance it

- Buy now, pay later

- Flex for approval

Social media only makes it worse. It tricks you into thinking everyone else has more, is doing better, and living some kind of perfect life. But what you don't see is how they paid for that vacation, that car, or that lifestyle. Credit cards? Loans? Strained relationships? Most people are unaware and that's the problem. The pressure to look successful is what traps most people and keeps them broke. Before you know it, you've fallen into the trap:

> You start spending tomorrow's money in order to feel good about yourself today.

As the data shows, most people finance their cars, max out their credit cards, lock themselves into payment plans, and engage in lifestyle inflation, chasing someone else's highlight reel and social media feed. It feels normal. It even feels necessary, but it's not wealth... it's a trap. The financial system doesn't care about your freedom, it cares about your spending. If you don't take control of your money, the system will gladly use you to keep itself running.

Social Media's Influence On Spending:

- Over half (57%) of social media users believe people post to look more successful, and 51% say social media promotes unrealistic lifestyles.

- Over a third of people admit to overspending to "keep up with the fun" they see on social media, and 40% of Gen Z are willing to spend more on experiences rather than necessities for the sake of sharing them online.

- $71 billion spent in 12 months on social media impulse buys.

- Consumers influenced by social media are 4x more likely to overspend.

So No, It's Not Your Fault...
You were never taught how money works.
You didn't get the tools, the strategy, or the truth.
You were trained to spend, not invest.
You were taught to survive, not build.
So no, this isn't about blame; this is about awareness.
Once you see it, once you understand it...
everything, including your behaviors change.

...But It Is Your Responsibility.
You're the CIO of You, Inc. now.
You're the one in charge.
You don't care about fault; you care about results.
What you do next is 100% on you.

Your Future Self Is Counting On You To Break The Cycle.
To stop hoping things will get better.
To start leading your life as it matters.
You don't have to fix everything overnight.
But you do have to act.

Because A.C.T. = Action Changes Things.
And your first actions?
Learning and thinking differently.
Seeing the trap and choosing a new path.
This workbook will give you the tools.
But only you can do the work.

Belief Flip:
Old belief: "The system is setup for me to lose, so I can't win."
New belief: "Yes, the system is rigged, but if I take control, I can still build wealth."

Chapter Four

The Money Monkey Trap

What Are You Holding That Has You Trapped?

I know this might sound a little crazy, but stick with me because this story is fascinating.

Old-school trappers used to catch monkeys in a way that says more about *us* than we may want to admit. Trappers would secure a coconut to a post and cut out a small hole, just big enough for a monkey to slip its hand inside. Then they'd bait it with something sweet: fruit, rice, or whatever the monkey couldn't resist.

When the monkey reached in and grabbed the treat, it couldn't pull its closed fist back out. Suddenly, the monkey realized that it was trapped. Ironically, its freedom was literally in its hands and all it had to do was **let go.** Inexplicably, it couldn't find the willpower to release the treat and reclaim its freedom. Even as the trapper approached, even as fear set in, the monkey refused to release what it was holding. It refused to let go of what was holding it captive. The bait became more valuable than its freedom.

Now pause for a second. Before you judge the monkey or start thinking, *"That's ridiculous,"* pause for a second and ask yourself:

What are you still holding that has you trapped?

Our "bait" looks different, but the behavior is the same. We grip things that feel like comfort, status, or success, but in reality, they're keeping us stuck. This is how the system keeps us trapped – it serves an endless supply of bait. Before we know it, we're caught in our own **money monkey trap** day after day.

There are seven main reasons we hold on, when we should let go:

    1. **Attachment to the behavior**: comfort in what's familiar.

    2. **Fear of loss:** believing release equals regret.

    3. **Short-term thinking:** chasing now over later.

4. **Deficit mindset:** focusing on lack instead of leverage.

5. **Resistance to change:** choosing comfort over growth.

6. **Ego and pride:** needing to look successful instead of *being* successful.

7. **Emotional decision-making:** letting feelings lead instead of principles.

Financial freedom requires release... Release of what isn't serving you well... Release of desires and choices that keep you poor. This is why being broke isn't your fault, but it's still your responsibility. Just as the monkey thinks the problem is the size of the hole in the coconut, most people believe the biggest problem is not enough income. With your hands stuck in the **money monkey trap**, you keep telling yourself that if only you made more money, everything would change. Here's what I've learned to be true:

Controlling spending can fix an income problem, but income can never fix a spending problem.

Expenses, debt and the choices you make determine if your hand remains stuck in the **money monkey trap.** I first learned this lesson at sixteen from my best friend's dad, Dr. Jackson. I once told him, "I want to make a lot of money like you." He smiled and said, "It's not about how much you make, it's about how much you spend." He was 100 percent right. It took me decades to really understand the profound nature of that statement. If you never learn to let go of the bait, the system will keep you trapped in a never-ending cycle of debt and distraction. If you feel financially stuck, ask yourself:

What am I holding on to that's keeping me trapped?

Because the moment you let go, that's the moment you're free to grow.

CIO Insight: Freedom Requires Release. You can't hold your future if your hands are full of the past. Every financial breakthrough begins with letting go of the habits, fears, or beliefs that keep you bound. The trap was never the coconut; it was the refusal to release what wasn't in the monkey's best interest.

Reflection Activity: Releasing the Bait
The Money Monkey Trap isn't really about monkeys, it's about mindset. Every one of us has something we keep grabbing that's holding us back. It might be a spending habit, a purchase that feeds our ego more than our goals, or a belief that says, *"If I just made more money, I'd be fine."*

Freedom starts when you decide to let go. On the following page, use the space to identify your "bait" and your release plan.

1. **Name Your Bait:**
   What's the one thing you keep holding onto that's keeping you financially stuck?
   (Example: a lifestyle you can't afford, emotional spending, expensive habits, fear of downsizing.)

2. **Why You Hold It:**
   What are you afraid will happen if you let go?
   (Example: feeling left out, losing status, confronting guilt or failure.)

3. **The Real Cost:**
   How is holding on to this "bait" costing you your freedom, peace, or progress?

4. **The Release Plan:**
   What step can you take this week to begin letting go?
   (Example: cancel a subscription, sell something unused, spend a weekend with no purchases.)

5. **Affirm the Lesson:**
   Write one line that reminds you of your new focus.
   (Example: "My freedom matters more than my image.")

Chapter Five

Should You Invest While In Debt?

You might be wondering: "Can I still invest if I have debt?" Or maybe it feels like it has to be either pay off debt or invest...The truth? It's not always either/or; it's about your strategy. This chapter (and book) isn't here to give you a one-size-fits-all answer; it's here to help you think like a CIO. That means weighing your interest rates, your cash flow, your psychology, and your long-term goals. Very likely, the most important question is: How do I build wealth and reduce risk, without losing momentum? Here are some things to consider:

Step 1: Know Your Numbers.
Ask yourself:

- What's the interest rate on your debt?

- What type of debt is it?

    ○ High-interest (credit cards, payday loans)?

    ○ Low-interest (student loans, mortgage)?

- What's your monthly cash flow?

    ○ Can you increase your income or reduce spending?

CIO Rule of Thumb: If your debt interest rate is above 7%, it's probably costing you more than most investments will earn.

Step 2: Your Quick-Glance Gameplan

Type of Debt	APR Range	Stackers Strategy
Credit Card	15–30%	Prioritize payoff. Invest only to employer match.
Personal Loan	8–14%	Pay down aggressively. Small investing okay.
Student Loan	4–7%	Split strategy. Pay minimum + start investing.
Mortgage	<5%	Invest freely. No need to accelerate payoff.

Step 3: Match Strategy to Mindset

Mindset	What to Focus On
"I need stability"	Focus on building a cash cushion first. Save at least one month of expenses to reduce stress before starting to invest.
"I need momentum"	Start investing a small amount now (even $25/mo) to build the habit while managing debt.
"I want balance"	Split your money: 80% to debt, 20% to investing. Reassess every 6 months.
"I need growth"	After paying minimums, put any extra cash toward long-term investing. This is where compounding lives.

Step 4: Run the Numbers.
Use a simple question: Should I pay off my debt faster or invest those funds?

Example:

Credit card debt at 28% → no brainer: pay it off

Student loan at 4.5% → investing at 8–10% makes sense

Step 5: Protect the Foundation.
Before you invest, build your launchpad. If this foundation isn't solid, investing is like building a house on sand and wondering why it keeps sinking. Here are the three core steps to create a stable foundation:

1. Build a starter emergency fund (at least $1,000)

2. Set up automatic minimum debt payments

3. Know your monthly net cash flow (what is left over after needs)

Don't wait until you're debt-free to start acting like an investor. That mindset shift is what moves you from spender to wealth builder. Some people need the peace of mind associated with being debt-free before investing and some need to start investing because that will motivate the shift from a spender. The key is to stay intentional, not emotional and know what will promote your success.

Example Hybrid Plan.

Let's say you have $300/month to work with:

• Put $200 toward high-interest debt

• Put $50 into a Roth IRA

• Save $50 in an emergency fund

Every 6 months:

• Reassess your interest rates, balances, and income

• Shift the ratio as needed to increase investing over time

Final Word: You Don't Have to Choose Debt or Investing
You can do both, just not equally over time. The key is to avoid thinking about this like a tug-of-war. Instead, view it as a balancing act. It's ok if the "math" says you should pay off debt first, and you decide on a hybrid approach because you know that will motivate you. Don't underestimate the importance of your psychology or the impact of emotions when it comes to money. Start where you are. Use what you have. Adjust as you grow.

Remember the power behind what you're doing isn't just your portfolio, it's your discipline, your identity, your future, and your lifelong relationship with money.

Chapter Six

The Lies You Were Sold About Wealth

B efore we build the truth, we need to uproot the lies. Most of us have been sold a version of wealth that isn't real, and it's cost you time, peace, confidence, and progress. It's no wonder so many people feel lost. American culture has been whispering (and sometimes screaming) false messages in your ear for years. Let's name them, uproot them, and replant with something better.

Lie #1: "You have to make a lot of money to build wealth."
This one keeps people stuck in silence, feeling like "until I make six figures, there's no point." According to LendingClub, as of 2023, 62% of Americans earning over $100,000 a year are living paycheck to paycheck. Let that sink in. Even with six figures coming in...most still feel broke. But here's the truth: *Wealth isn't about how much you make; it's about how much you keep.*

> Or as my "other Dad" told me: "It's not about how much you make, it's about how much you spend."
> Or as Jim Rohn said: "When your outflow exceeds your income, your upkeep becomes your downfall."

Lie #2: "You need to know everything before you start."
Wrong again. Wealth is built through action and you don't need to know every acronym, read every book, or wait until "you feel ready." You'll never feel ready enough to begin. You just need to start. Learn a little. Act a little. Repeat. Successful investors aren't the ones with perfect timing; they're the ones who got in the game and stayed in. It's amazing how much more you learn during the process once you start.

Lie #3: "Investing is only for rich people."
This is one of the most dangerous myths out there, because it convinces people that the game of investing isn't for them, so they stay out of it. But the truth is, the sooner you start, the sooner you can become one of those rich people. You don't need thousands. You don't need a stockbroker. You don't need anything other than the will to start and continue learning. Make the decision.

Lie #4: "If you were smart, you'd already have this figured out."
This lie is cruel. This turns lack of knowledge into shame. If you're like most people, you were never exposed to this growing up. This wasn't discussed at home, at school, or anywhere. Suddenly, you're just supposed to know it all? Be kind to yourself! Everything is hard when you first try it.

Lie #5: "Wealth is about looking successful."
This is the biggest wealth killer, and it's heartbreaking. Countless dreams of financial freedom have been sacrificed at the altar of this lie: you have to look rich to feel worthy. The irony? People are drowning in debt just to avoid looking broke. Real wealth? It's quiet. It's patient. It's invisible on purpose.

Too many people spend money to impress folks they don't care about, people who probably don't care about them either, and definitely don't enjoy seeing them do well. Whether it's to feel accepted, to look successful, or to silence insecurity, chasing status through spending is a trap. Whatever it is they're chasing (acceptance, belonging, confidence, comfort), it doesn't come from outside of you and it definitely doesn't come with a monthly payment.

> True wealth isn't loud, and it doesn't flex. It's the quiet confidence of knowing you don't owe anyone anything.

The Truth
- Wealth is about assets. Being broke is about liabilities.

- Liabilities are what people see.

- Wealth is invisible.

- Wealth quietly compounds in the background while everyone is busy showing off.

- Building wealth starts the moment you decide to stop believing the lies and start building your truth.

What Is Wealth (Really)?
One of the biggest problems for people is they talk about wealth without defining it. That definition will very likely be different for each person. My preferred definition for wealth is: "Wealth is the ability to live how you want, without money being the reason why you can't do something." That's it. It's not just about how much you make. It's about how much time, freedom, and options you really have. Understanding that money is an important part of that equation...More on that later.

Wealth and the rich are not the same. Being rich is about money coming in, while wealth is about what stays, what grows, and what works for you when you're not working. When you frame it this way, wealth isn't just measured in dollars; it's measured in how long you could live off your assets without earning another dime.

That's the test. This is why you must view every dollar as an employee and why you must ensure they work harder than you do. Investing isn't just about building a bank account; it's about building today the life you desire tomorrow. It's about being able to walk away from the job that drains you. It's about being able to say "yes" to the things that matter and "no" to the things that don't. When you understand wealth this way, you start building with intention and resist the temptation to consume more...to need less...to stress less...and to live more.

Belief Flip: You Can't Save Your Way to Financial Freedom

Most people were taught one financial message their whole life: "Just save your money." Why? While the ability to save is critical, it's almost like putting a cake in the oven and not turning the oven on. Saving preserves what you have and protects your investments in cases of an emergency. When you save, you're accumulating money. When you invest, you're multiplying your money. In a world with inflation, rising costs, and a system designed to keep you spending, saving alone is not enough.

Beliefs are invisible systems. They run the show whether you're aware of them or not. The goal of this section is to rewrite that hidden code and replace outdated beliefs with the mindset of a true Chief Investment Officer. To build real wealth, you need to shift from just saving to investing with intention and compounding. That's where Belief Flips come in. These are the outdated ideas you were taught and the new beliefs we're choosing instead.

Belief Flips That Change Everything

Old Belief	New Belief
Saving is the safest thing I can do.	Investing smartly is what protects and multiplies my future.
I need to save a lot before I start investing.	I can start small and build consistent investing habits now.
If I don't touch it, I'm doing the right thing.	If I don't grow it, I'll always be behind.
I'll invest once I make more money.	Investing is how I'll make more money in the future.
Risk is bad.	Risk is necessary and must be managed, not avoided.
I'm not smart enough to invest.	I'm smart enough to learn and I'm starting right now.
Wealth is for other people.	Wealth is something I'm actively building.

Chapter Seven

Every Dollar Is An Employee...

Are Your Employees Working Hard?

One of the most significant mindset shifts you'll ever make is how you perceive money. Different groups think about money in completely different ways:

- The poor see money as something to spend, usually on things that bring comfort or status.

- The middle class sees money as a way to pay bills and maintain good credit, so they can qualify to buy more things.

- The wealthy see money as a tool to multiply so that they can buy freedom, time, and legacy.

Until you shift how you see money, you'll keep repeating the same patterns, just with different numbers.

Every dollar is an employee and the question is: are they working hard? Or are they just wandering around doing nothing? This shift means you're not just spending, you're hiring. Imagine it this way, every time money hits your account; it clocks in. As the CIO, the boss, you must make sure your employees are assigned to three key areas:

- Growth (Investments)

- Protection (Emergency fund, insurance)

- Serving (Donations, giving)

If you don't give your dollars a job, they will move around without direction and find a way to spend themselves. When you review where your money goes, it's really telling you about your priorities. For example, you can't say you value freedom when your money keeps chasing entertainment. This is why you need clarity and a clear purpose, not because you will be perfect, but to make sure what you do with your money reflects your values, goals, and dreams. Later in this guide, you'll learn about how to automate your flow, track your cash, and build a system that runs on autopilot. For now, start by seeing your dollars as the employees and tools they are for building wealth.

Chapter Eight

Now Hiring: Chief Investment Officer (CIO) of You, Inc.

Position Summary

Y ou, Inc. is seeking a highly motivated and values-driven leader to serve as Chief Investment Officer (CIO). In this pivotal role, the employee will manage all financial strategies, ensuring that every dollar invested aligns with the company's long-term goals. You will be responsible for guiding investments that drive sustainable wealth creation and contribute to financial freedom, all while promoting steady progress toward the broader mission of wealth and independence.

Reports To: The Board of You, Inc. (that's you, and your family if applicable)

Location: Everywhere you go

Hours: 24/7 awareness...about 10 hours per month of active learning and management

Core Responsibilities:
- Assign dollar employees to productive roles that create value.

- Build and maintain simple financial systems (automation, cash flow, review).

- Conduct monthly reviews of financial records, net worth, and progress.

- Direct investments with patience and discipline, not emotion.

- Protect the enterprise against risk and distraction.

- Lead financial decisions with clarity, confidence, and purpose.

Minimum Qualifications:
- Willingness to learn and apply financial fundamentals.

- Ability to track 3–5 key numbers monthly (cash flow, savings rate, net worth, contributions).

- Commitment to spend at least 10 hours a month on reviews and learning.

- No prior degree required: curiosity and consistency are the only prerequisites.

Education:
- A growth mindset.

- A willingness to keep learning and improving.

- Patience to let compound growth work over time.

Compensation & Benefits:
- Reduced money stress and confusion.

- Clear direction for financial decisions.

- A growing net worth over time.

- Confidence in leading your financial future.

- Freedom to build the life you want.

Equal Opportunity Statement:
You, Inc. does not discriminate based on past mistakes, income level, or when you began your journey. The only requirement is that you take the first step today.

Next Step:
If this sounds like the right fit, turn the page to review your official offer letter and sign on as CIO of You, Inc.

Chapter Nine

You're Hired

Chief Investment Officer Contract – Effective Immediately

Congratulations! You've been selected as the Chief Investment Officer of You, Inc. because of your willingness to learn and your commitment to growth. Your engagement with *The Beginner's Guide to Investing & Growing Wealth* shows you're serious about building a better financial future. You've already shown the courage to break old patterns and the curiosity to build new ones. That initiative qualifies you for this role – and today, we're making it official.

A promise only matters if it's personal. Before you sign this contract, take a breath and realize you're declaring independence from financial survival mode.

This role is vital because wealth is not built by chance; it's built by leadership with intentionality. Every dollar is an employee, and without direction, those employees drift. As CIO, you are responsible for assigning each dollar a role, holding it accountable, and ensuring it contributes to your long-term goals. This is how you move from staying busy to building true wealth. This is how you shift from surviving to thriving.

You display the exact qualities of a phenomenal CIO: curiosity, discipline, and a willingness to take ownership. You don't need a finance degree or a Wall Street pedigree. What sets you apart is your mindset, the readiness and willingness to lead your financial life with clarity and purpose.

Compensation & Benefits
Your compensation will not come in the form of paychecks, but in the outcomes. By leading with intention, you will experience less financial stress, greater confidence in your decisions, measurable growth in savings and investments, and the freedom to design life on your terms. These benefits compound the longer you stay in office, turning leadership into lasting wealth.

Term
This contract begins today and has no expiration date. Your appointment as CIO continues as long as you choose to lead. No renewal forms. No probationary period. Just your ongoing commitment to show up and guide your financial future with consistency.

Acceptance
By signing below, you acknowledge your appointment as Chief Investment Officer of You, Inc. and agree to lead your financial future with clarity, consistency, and purpose.

Signed:

Date:

Transition: From Identity to Action
Congratulations! By signing your offer letter, you didn't just imagine yourself as the CIO of You, Inc.; you made it official. That signature was your first executive act. You've broken the ground, claimed the role, and now it's time to step into the work. Like any new leader, your journey begins with orientation. The assignments that follow are your first responsibilities as CIO. They're designed to give you clarity, build confidence, and help you take immediate ownership of your financial workforce. This isn't busywork. These are the first real moves of your leadership, the actions that transform intention into momentum.

Welcome to your first day on the job. Let's get to work.

Chapter Ten

Tools

Activity #1: Employee Audit - Who's On Your Payroll?

I f every dollar is an employee, then your money is your workforce. Then the question becomes: Are you running a business that builds wealth, or one that's busy confusing activity with accomplishments and ends up with no profit? In any healthy business, employees have roles, responsibilities, and accountability. Productive employees generate value, unproductive ones drain resources, and unmanaged ones can quietly walk out the back door. Your dollars work the same way.

This activity will help you audit your financial workforce. In Step 1, by filling in the table, you'll see which of your dollar employees are driving momentum toward your goals and which are showing up without adding value, or worse, costing you. The goal is to stop confusing activity with accomplishment and start leading your money like a business that exists to grow.

Step 1: Fill Out The Table
- **Category:** Review each category of spending.

- **Examples:** Use these to guide your thinking (Roth IRA, rent, tithes, restaurants, etc.).

- **How Much Per Month?** Write down the actual dollar amount you currently spend in each category.

- **How Do You Feel About It?** Be honest. Do you feel proud, stressed, guilty, uncertain, or motivated?

(Tip: Don't aim for perfection here, just capture where your dollars are really going. Awareness is the first step toward change.)

Category	Examples	How Much Per Month?	How Do You Feel About It?
Investing & Wealth Building	Roth IRA, 401(k), brokerage account, real estate, etc.		
Protection & Peace	Emergency fund, insurance, savings buffer		
Growth & Education	Courses, coaching, tools that expand knowledge or skill		
Essentials & Needs	Rent, food, transportation, utilities		
Giving & Generosity	Tithes, donations, helping family/friends		
Lifestyle & Fun	Restaurants, clothes, subscriptions, entertainment		
Untracked or Unaligned	Impulse buys, subscriptions you forgot, unnecessary fees		

Step 2: Reflect and Journal

- After completing the table, step back and ask yourself:

- Which category is over-employed (too many dollars working there)?

- Which category is underfunded (not enough dollars assigned)?

- Where are your dollars clearly working hard?

- Where are they just hanging out or wasting time?

Then write your reflections:

- As the CIO of You, Inc., where are you leading well?

- Where do you need to make a change?

- What's one step you can take today to reassign at least one of your dollar employees to a more productive role?

Activity #2: Success Is More Than a Number

Too many people chase income goals without asking: "What would that money actually do for me"?

- Is it about peace of mind?

- Is it about freedom of time?

- Is it about being able to say "yes" to the things that matter... and "no" to the things that don't?

Success isn't about having more.
It's about having enough to live aligned with your values.

This workbook isn't about helping you get rich; it's about helping you get free. Thankfully, freedom looks different for everyone:

- For some, it's retiring early.

- For others, it's paying off a home.

- For you, it might be traveling more, giving more, or simply sleeping better at night.

Whatever it is, you must own it. When you define success clearly, you can stop chasing, stop comparing, and start building.

Reflection Prompt:
- What does financial success look like for me?

- How will I know I'm living it, not just earning it?

- What do I want my money to do for my life?

Activity #3: Success Is More Than A Number

You're not just earning a living; you're stepping into your role as the CIO, and every successful business has a clear mission. It's time to write your mission statement, the guiding vision behind every financial decision you'll make moving forward. This is your anchor, your filter, and your North Star. Don't worry about making it perfect. Just make it real, personal, and deeply meaningful.

Step 1: Reflect on Your "Why"
Use these questions to clarify what really matters to you:

- What kind of life do I want to build?

- Who am I doing this for...besides myself?

- What will financial freedom allow me to do, feel, or give?

- What values do I want my money to reflect?

Step 2: Draft Your Mission Statement
Your mission should answer: "Why am I leading my financial life on purpose?"
Use this fill-in-the-blank if it helps:

> "As the CIO of my life, my mission is to build a future where (FILL-IN) by leading my money with (FILL-IN) and aligning my decisions with (FILL IN)." Or write your own version.

Final Thought
You don't need to frame it or post it on the wall (unless you want to), but let this mission guide you when you feel tired, distracted, or uncertain. When you know why you're building wealth, you'll stay focused long enough to actually build it.

STAGE 2

PLANTING THE SEEDS

Chapter Eleven

Introduction: Planting the Seeds

Theme: Knowledge Takes Root Goal: Understand investing fundamentals and begin building your inner strategy.

*N*ow that the soil is ready, it's time to plant! This stage provides the seeds of true financial understanding: what investing truly is, how money grows, and how to identify the silent threats, such as inflation, that erode your wealth. You'll start to understand concepts like ROI, compound interest, asset classes, and diversification, but through the eyes of a CIO.

You're not memorizing facts. You're building a philosophy – a playbook.

Each chapter is a seed. Some will grow quickly in your mind; others will take time. But all of them are chosen to help you grow strong, sustainable financial roots. Remember, you don't need to master everything overnight. You're not cramming for a test; you're preparing for a harvest.

Learn the Game, So You Can Play to Win

Investing isn't just about putting your money somewhere and hoping it grows sometime down the road. You need a real strategy to make it happen. Here's the reality: most people don't lose the wealth game because they're lazy; they lose because they don't know the rules and how the game is played.

In this section, we're making the game make sense and giving you the knowledge to win by showing you:

- What investing really is (not what Wall Street wants you to think it is)

- Why saving alone won't get you free

- How time and compound growth are your unfair advantages

- How inflation is quietly robbing your future

- What the different asset classes are (and how they work together)

- How to manage risk like a pro

- And why diversification and ROI aren't just buzzwords, instead they're part of your winning formula

This is where confidence starts to grow, and you begin trusting that you can truly be the CIO.

Chapter Twelve

What Is Investing (Really)?

It's Not Just About Making Money, It's About Making Moves

The myth we need to destroy is that investing is what you do after you've paid your bills. The rich and wealthy invest FIRST and live off the rest. Investing is not what they do with their "extra" or leftover cash. Investing is how you become rich, not just in dollars, but in time, options, and purpose.

> The Real Definition: Investing is the act of allocating resources today (money, time, energy) in order to create greater value tomorrow.

Notice that the resources are time, energy, and money. If you're like most people, you have more time than money right now. This is why you should always start by investing your time in learning. Benjamin Franklin said it best, "An investment in knowledge pays the best interest."

Here's the next shift:

- You're not just buying stocks.

- You're not just funding a retirement account.

- You're managing, directing, and allocating your employees like a boss to make sure your employees produce the best possible results (returns) for your level of risk

Spending vs Investing:
One of the biggest tug-of-wars is spending vs investing. While we all have to spend to support our lives, every dollar above that baseline becomes a dollar you can't invest. This is a major mindset shift. It doesn't mean you have to live a life of lack, unable to spend money on a date or a night out. It is a way to acknowledge that the biggest challenge for most people is finding the dollars to invest. The way you win this tug-of-war is through intentionality. It's not about sacrificing things; it's about intentionally deciding what to do with each of your dollars. Do they get

spent on things, or do they stay with you and go to work by growing your wealth? This is how you start making moves with your money. The poor and working poor believe that money is primarily about paying bills and maintaining their lifestyle, whereas the rich view it as a means to generate more wealth, which in turn supports their lifestyle. The average consumer buys things to feel something.

The CIO invests to build something.

Investing is a behavior, not a product. Don't let Wall Street fool you into thinking investing is about having access to fancy products. It's not. Later, you will see that most people only need to invest in 2-3 boring index funds. Wall Street and its brokers want you to think that investing is about managed accounts, with specialized products that promise exceptional returns. Investing is about a behavior – a rhythm – a pattern of choices made consistently, uninterrupted over time so that it can grow and compound. As we will discuss next, this is why time is your superpower.

When it comes to investing, there are 5 main investments you should consider:

- Yourself - education, skills, health

- Your business: time, attention, systems

- Other people's businesses: stocks, private equity, partnerships

- Assets: real estate, metals, crypto, collectibles

- Your future: retirement accounts, index funds, life insurance

CIO Insight: Investing is how you move from a life of reaction to a life of design. When you choose to invest, you're saying, "I believe my future is worth building and I trust myself to lead it." That's not a financial transaction; it's about assuming the leadership role for your financial life.

Quick Exercise: Write this down somewhere you'll see it: **"My money doesn't just work hard; it works hard for me."** That's the energy you're keeping going forward.

Chapter Thirteen

Time Is Your Superpower

Here's the thing nobody tells you: You don't need more money; you need more time with your money. For example, what's better? Investing $100 per month starting at 25 or $500 a month starting at 45? It's the difference between having $535K and $347K. The 45-year-old invested 5 times as much as the 25-year-old, but because of time, the older investor ends up with significantly less. This is what turns regular people into millionaires. Not income. Not luck. Good old-fashioned TIME.

"Time can't be borrowed, bought, or hacked, but when you respect and leverage it, it can do amazing things." This table says it all:

Starting Age	Years to Invest	Monthly Contribution	Contributions	Future Total (10% Interest)
25	40	$200/month	$96,200	$1,071, 273
35	30	$550/month	$198,550.00	$1,095,257
45	20	$1,550/month	$373,550	$1,075,742
55	10	$5,550/month	$665,500	$1,066,135

- Start at 25? That's an inexpensive car lease: $200/month and you're on the million-dollar track.

- Wait till 35? You have to more than double that.

- Start at 45? Now it's rent money.

- Wait till 55? You'd better be ready to stack heavy...or praying for a bull market miracle.

CIO Insight: You don't need a lot of money; you need a lot of time. Time isn't just a resource; it's leverage. Time allows your money time to do more and more work with less effort. Every year you wait, the cost of wealth increases. Every month you delay, the opportunity cost compounds. If you've let some time slip through your fingers, don't worry, we'll talk about how to catch up. The investing game rewards those who start early and stay consistent, because of what Albert Einstein called the "Eighth Wonder of the World": compound interest.

Why Time Beats Talent, Tools, or Even Timing

Compound interest/growth: All time is not created equal! The secret behind time is compound interest/growth. This is when your money earns money - then that money earns more interest (money) – and then that money earns even more interest (money). It's interest on interest. Gains on gains. It's stacking on autopilot. Many of us have heard of the snowball method for addressing debt, well; this is the snowball method for growing wealth. Here's a simple example:

- If you invest $100 and it earns 10% per year, then after year one, you have $110. That's your original $100 plus $10 in interest. But here's where things start to shift..

- In year two, your 10% return isn't just on your original $100; it's on the full $110 (your initial investment plus the $10 you already earned). Now, instead of earning $10 again, you earn $11.

- At the end of year two, you have $121 and the snowball keeps growing from there.

It doesn't sound like a lot, because you haven't used your superpower...TIME!

The Compounding Snowball: Think of investing like rolling a snowball down a hill. At first, it's small and slow. As it rolls, it builds momentum and collects more snow. The longer the ball is allowed to roll downhill (a.k.a. time), the bigger the snowball becomes, like exponentially bigger. Most wealth is lost or never made because the biggest growth happens later in time. You don't see big results in the first few years which makes it so easy for most people to give up too early. This is where the Rule of 72 comes in.

The Rule of 72: The Formula Every CIO Should Know

72 ÷ interest rate = years to double your money. For example, if you earn an average return of 8% per year:

- $72 \div 8 = 9$

- That means your money doubles roughly every 9 years

Now imagine this:

- $10,000 at 8% becomes $20,000 in 9 years

- Then $40,000 in another 9

- Then $80,000... then $160,000...

- All without adding a single dollar

That doesn't feel like math; it feels like Harry Potter sorcery, casting a spell on time: Tempus Reverter. Even if you're 40, 50, or 60, the game isn't over. You may not have 40 years left to grow your money, but you do have enough time to make strategic moves. The sooner you start, the stronger your position becomes.

CIO Insight: Every dollar you invest today has more earning potential than a dollar you invest next year. Do not waste time trying to "get it perfect." Start where you are, with what you have, because time compounds too, not just money.

Discipline compounds.
Wisdom compounds.
Confidence compounds.

Quick Exercise: Write a response to this: "What small action(s) can I take today that my future self will thank me for 10 years from now?"

Chapter Fourteen

Inflation: The Silent Thief

If Your Money Isn't Growing, It's Shrinking

Here's the brutal truth most people ignore: if your money isn't growing faster than inflation, you're getting poorer every day, every year.

The rich and wealthy understand this very well. You may feel like you're playing it safe by letting your money sit in a savings account, but in reality, you're bleeding purchasing power. Slowly. Quietly. Relentlessly. Inflation is that silent thief sneaking into your financial house, year after year, stealing your future buying power. Most people won't notice until they can no longer afford to retire or their lifestyle has changed. That's not a fluke; this is how the system is built.

Over the last few years, Americans have become painfully aware of inflation's sting, especially at the grocery store, gas pump, and housing market. The 2% targeted inflation rate often goes unnoticed year-over-year as your money slowly buys less and less. Inflation is like running on a treadmill that keeps speeding up. **This is exactly why you can't save your way to wealth. If you're not investing, you're not standing still, you're sliding backward.**

The chart below shows what dollar decay looks like. Over the last century, the U.S. dollar has quietly lost over 90% of its purchasing power. Inflation is simply a nice way of referencing the erosion of the dollar. This chart tracks one simple question: *How many sodas could $1 buy in each decade?* It's a visual punchline to a painful truth: *Saving alone isn't safe, holding cash is losing value.* Further proof that investing isn't a luxury.

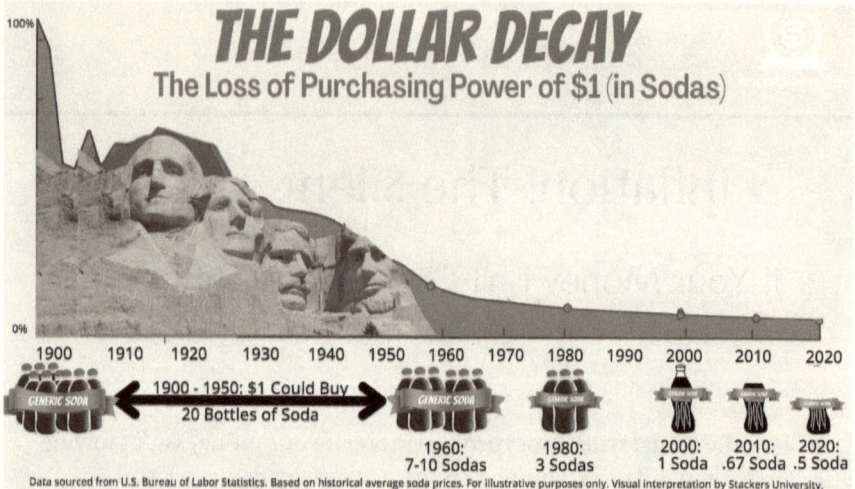

THE DOLLAR DECAY
The Loss of Purchasing Power of $1 (in Sodas)

100%

0%

1900 1910 1920 1930 1940 1950 1960 1970 1980 1990 2000 2010 2020

GENERIC SODA   1900 - 1950: $1 Could Buy   GENERIC SODA   GENERIC SODA
20 Bottles of Soda

1960:   1980:   2000:   2010:   2020:
7-10 Sodas   3 Sodas   1 Soda   .67 Soda   .5 Soda

Data sourced from U.S. Bureau of Labor Statistics. Based on historical average soda prices. For illustrative purposes only. Visual interpretation by Stackers University.

The Goal: Outpace Inflation

The job of every Chief Investment Officer is to beat inflation over time. Savings accounts? Usually lose to inflation. Basic bonds? Sometimes lose to inflation. Index funds, real estate, and productive assets historically win. For clarification, you don't need to take on excessive risk to outpace inflation, but you do need to take educated, intentional action so your dollars don't lose purchasing power.

> **CIO Insight:** The longer you wait to invest, the more ground you'll have to make up. This isn't about fear; it's about urgency with purpose. You don't fight inflation by stressing; you fight it by taking action and investing.

> **Quick Exercise:** Make a short list of things you've noticed getting more expensive over the last 5 years. Then ask yourself: "What would it take for my money to keep up with that?" Your investing journey just got a mission: Don't let the thief win.

Chapter Fifteen

The Investor's Toolbox

Your Essential Tools for Building Wealth

WARNING: Boring but Critical Information to Follow!

Alright, CIO of You, Inc., let's talk tools. Asset classes are the parts that make up your financial vehicle. Each serves a purpose as some protect, some grow and some stabilize. This is the longest and most technical chapter in this guide, for good reason. It's also not the most exciting read, but it's the chapter that unlocks every action you'll take afterward. Think of it like a bootcamp: tough but transformative. You're stepping into the driver's seat of your financial life. And to drive your vehicle well?

You need to be familiar with the key components and parts. It's technical. It's long. And it's exactly what makes this guide different from the fluff out there. If you can get through this, you will have earned your Top CIO Badge.

***

A. Cash & Cash Equivalents: The Emergency Brake
This is your "oh snap" money. Easy to access, low risk, and boring...in the best possible way.

- **Savings Accounts:** Earn less than 1% interest, barely beat inflation. FDIC insured.

- **High-Yield Savings Accounts (HYSA):** A better version of savings accounts. FDIC insured.

- **Certificates of Deposit (CDs):** Lock in cash for a set period. Penalties for early withdrawals. FDIC insured.

- **Money Market Accounts:** Hybrid savings and checking. Usually FDIC or NCUA insured, always check with your bank or credit union.

- **Money Market Funds:** Similar to MMAs, but offered by investment firms. Not FDIC insured. Always read the prospectus.

Purpose: Safety. Liquidity. Not growth. You access this in emergencies, as it's not for building wealth, but for providing protection instead.

CIO Quick Take: These accounts won't make you rich. However, they will help you avoid going broke.

***

B. Stocks (Equities): The Engine
Owning stock = owning part of a company. This is the growth machine of your portfolio.

- Common vs Preferred: Common = more upside and voting rights.

- Preferred = stable dividends.

- Growth vs Value: Growth = fast-growing companies. Value = companies trading at a discount to earnings.

How They Make You Money:

- Appreciation: Stock price goes up.

- Dividends: The company pays you part of its profit.

The Stock Market: Beyond the Big Screen
You've seen the stock market in movies, right? Ignore that, the real stock market is a bit more complex (and a whole lot less dramatic). Think of the stock market as a giant online flea market, but instead of selling old toys and furniture, people are buying and selling pieces of companies (stocks). Companies need money, so issuing stocks is one way they generate the income needed to grow, expand, or develop new products.

- IPO: You might have heard the phrase, "Initial Public Offering." This is when a company first offers shares to the public. It's like opening the doors to the flea market for the first time.

- Exchanges: The stock market is organized into exchanges. The two major exchanges in the U.S. are the New York Stock Exchange (NYSE) and the NASDAQ. These exchanges provide a place for buyers and sellers to transact. Other major exchanges outside the U.S. include:

  - Tokyo Stock Exchange (TSE) - Japan

  - Shanghai Stock Exchange (SSE) - China

  - Hong Kong Stock Exchange (HKEX) - Hong Kong

  - London Stock Exchange (LSE) - United Kingdom

  - Toronto Stock Exchange (TSX) - Canada

  - Australian Securities Exchange (ASX) - Australia

How Does The "Market" Work?

- **Supply and Demand:** This drives stock prices; if more people want to buy a stock than sell it, the price goes up. If more people want to sell than buy, the price goes down.

- **Investors:** People who buy and sell stocks are called investors. They can be individuals or big institutions like pension funds, hedge funds, and insurance companies.

- **Brokerage Accounts:** This is where you buy and sell stocks and other assets. It's almost like a bank account specifically for investing.

- **Orders:** When you want to buy or sell a stock, you place an order through your brokerage account. There are different types of orders, but only two for beginners:

  - Market Order: Buy or sell the stock at the current market price.

  - Limit Order: Buy or sell the stock at a specific price.

- **Fluctuations:** Stock prices can fluctuate wildly for a variety of reasons: company news, economic data, company earnings, investor sentiment, or even rumors.

Understanding U.S. Market Indexes

Market indexes (and index funds) are like scorecards for the stock market. They track the performance of a group of stocks, giving you a sense of how the overall market or a specific segment of the market is doing. There are indexes that track specific sectors (like technology or healthcare), specific regions (like emerging markets), or even specific investment strategies (like socially responsible investing). Here are some of the major indexes you'll often hear about:

- Dow Jones Industrial Average (DJIA): Often called "the Dow," it tracks 30 large, well-known U.S. companies. It's a limited snapshot of the market, but widely reported.

- S&P 500 (Standard & Poor's 500): Tracks 500 of the largest publicly traded companies in the U.S. It's considered a broader and more representative measure of the U.S. stock market than the Dow.

- NASDAQ Composite: Includes over 2,500 stocks listed on the Nasdaq exchange, with a heavy weighting towards technology companies.

- Russell 2000: Tracks the performance of 2,000 small-cap (small company) stocks in the U.S. It's a good indicator of how smaller companies are doing.

> **TL;DR:** Individual stocks, ETFs (exchange traded funds – discussed later), and index funds are traded on exchanges (NYSE or NASDAQ) and purchased through your brokerage account. An index (S&P 500, Russell 2000, etc.) is a cluster of companies based on certain criteria. An index fund is designed to track the index it follows.

Understanding International and Emerging Markets

Beyond the U.S. stock market, there's a whole world of investment opportunities. Investing internationally can offer diversification and exposure to potentially faster-growing economies.

- Developed International Markets: The MSCI EAFE index is a common benchmark for this area.

- Emerging Markets: These are the markets of developing countries.

> **TL;DR:** As a beginner, you just need to know they exist and offer diversification, typically with more risk.

Purpose: This is the primary growth aspect of your portfolio. Your ownership of stocks offers the potential for long-term appreciation and passive income through dividends. The potential growth comes with some higher levels of risk (loss of investment).

CIO Quick Take: Equities are where your money stops sitting and starts working. This is how you beat inflation. Your job isn't to pick the next big winner; it's to stay consistent, and let time do the heavy lifting.

***

C. Bonds (Debt Instruments): The Shock Absorbers

When you buy a bond, you're basically lending money to a company or the government, and they "promise" to pay back with interest. Typically, the longer the period of time, the higher the interest rate. Think of them like shock absorbers because they aren't exciting, but they provide stability and dampen the ups and downs in your car and portfolio.

What Are the Different Types of Bonds?

- U.S. Treasury Bonds: Low risk, low return.

- Municipal Bonds: Often tax-free, used for city/state projects.

- Corporate Bonds: Higher yield = higher risk.

- High-Yield (Junk) Bonds: Riskier companies, bigger returns/losses.

- Emerging Market Bonds: Issued by governments or corporations in developing countries, typically offering higher yields and higher risk.

- Mortgage-Backed Securities: Bonds backed by pools of mortgages, providing exposure to real estate markets.

Purpose: Stability. Bonds don't accelerate your car — but they keep you from flying off the road.

How Bonds Work?

The language around bonds can feel very confusing at first (take a deep breath). When you buy a bond, the entity agrees to pay back the original amount (called the "face value") on a specific date ("maturity date"). The interest you receive from your bond is called the "coupon," which is a fixed percentage of the face value which results in what you earn ("yield").

For example, a 2-year (maturity date), $1,000 bond (face value) with a 5% coupon (interest rate) pays you $50 (yield) per year until maturity. At maturity, your face value ($1,000) will be returned.

Bond Prices and Interest Rates (AKA Yields)

Think back to the playground when you and a friend sat on a see-saw (teeter-totter). When one of you went down to the ground, the other person went higher in the air. Interest rates and bond prices do the same thing; they move in opposite directions. When market interest rates go up, the value of existing bonds goes down, and vice versa. This is because new bonds may offer higher coupons (interest rates), making older bonds with lower coupons (interest rates) less attractive unless their price drops.

> **TL;DR:** Bonds typically provide stability to your account. It is widely accepted that as you age you continue to increase your bond allocation.

Purpose: They don't deliver the excitement or returns of high-growth assets, but they play a critical role in stabilizing your portfolio, smoothing out volatility, and offering predictable income, especially when the market gets rocky.

CIO Quick Take: Bonds aren't about building wealth; they protect it by generating moderate levels of income.

***

D. Mutual Funds and ETFs: The Automatic Transmission

Keeping with the car analogy, mutual funds and ETFs are like having an automatic transmission; they make investing much easier, less work, and more enjoyable. They can hold a mix of stocks, bonds, and other investments. They are managed in one of two ways:

1. By a professional manager (actively managed accounts) who drives the investment decisions

or

2. Passively managed accounts aren't managed by anyone in particular.

These funds typically track the performance of a market index, such as the S&P 500, by holding the same securities in the same proportions as the index. Exchange-Traded Funds (ETFs) are similar to mutual funds, except they trade like stocks on an exchange and offer greater flexibility compared to mutual funds.

Mutual Fund and ETF Cost Considerations

The four most important considerations are: expense ratios, sales fees/commissions, trading costs, and taxes. In a nutshell, these fees eat away at your returns and profits, especially over time. For most investors, it is best to utilize passively managed accounts that track broad indexes. Research shows that most actively managed funds underperform the major indexes.

Purpose: Simplicity and diversification. Mutual funds and ETFs let you invest in dozens or even hundreds of assets at once, giving you instant diversification and a smoother ride, without needing to hand-pick every stock. They're one of the easiest ways to start investing while reducing risk and saving time.

CIO Quick Take: Mutual funds and ETFs take the guesswork out of investing. Instead of trying to pick winners, you're buying the whole race and letting time do the heavy lifting. For most beginners (and even many pros), broad-market ETFs are the smart default. Low cost, low maintenance, high leverage. Set it, forget it, and let it stack.

***

E. Real Estate (Not Your Home): The Frame
Like the frame on your car, real estate can support and stabilize your financial goals. Real estate (residential or commercial) is a highly loved investment because it can provide a steady stream of passive income (tax advantaged), while also offering the potential for long-term appreciation as the property's value increases. In addition, investors benefit from various tax advantages, such as deductions for mortgage interest, property taxes, repairs, and depreciation (a "phantom" expense), which can help reduce taxable income.

Some investors avoid the landlord aspect by buying and flipping properties, while others invest in REITs (Real Estate Investment Trusts). REITs serve as a hands-off way to gain real estate exposure. Think of a REIT like a mutual fund for real estate, letting you benefit from property ownership while bypassing the landlord role and managing tenants. By law, REITs must distribute at least 90% of their taxable income to shareholders in the form of dividends, making them a reliable income stream for many investors. The recommendation is that you invest your time learning about real estate long before you invest your money.

Purpose: Growth, income, and diversification. Real estate isn't just about owning property; the key is creating a cash-flowing asset that works for you while you sleep. Regardless of the type you choose, it can strengthen your portfolio with steady income, long-term appreciation, and powerful tax advantages.

CIO Quick Take: Real estate can build wealth, or it can absolutely drain it. Don't get caught up in the "passive income" hype. It's becomes passive only after a lot of learning, planning, and hustle. You don't have to be a landlord to be a real estate investor... but you do need to be a student of the game before you step on the field.

***

F. Commodities and Precious Metals: The Insurance Policy or Spare Tire
In full disclosure, precious metals are one of the Doc's favorite asset classes because they are like an insurance policy or spare tire; you forget about them until you need them, and when you need them, you're glad you have them. Investing in other commodities such as oil, gas and agricultural products offers another way to diversify your portfolio, often serving as a hedge against inflation or economic uncertainty. When it comes to precious metals, specifically gold and silver, Doc strongly recommends a certain allocation to the physical metals in your possession.

Purpose: Commodities and precious metals serve as a counterweight to traditional stocks. They shine when the rest of your portfolio stumbles. In particular, they offer upside during periods of inflation, geopolitical tension, and economic uncertainty. These assets don't move in sync with equities, which makes them powerful during market cycles. You don't need them to perform consistently, just when it matters most. Precious metals in particular, help protect your purchasing power over time.

CIO Quick Take: Every CIO needs a spare tire. Gold and silver won't always win the race, but when the system breaks down, they'll help you keep moving forward. Don't stack for the hype, stack for the hedge and cyclical performance. When it comes to metals? If you don't hold it, you don't own it (or at least hold some of it).

***

G. Cryptocurrencies: The High-Octane Turbocharger
Cryptocurrency is like adding a turbocharger to your engine: it's fast, volatile, and not always predictable, but when used wisely, it can give your portfolio a serious boost. Think of crypto as digital money, powered by decentralized technology (blockchain) and unregulated by traditional financial systems.

Bitcoin is the OG, viewed by many as "digital gold." Ethereum adds smart contracts and utility. And beyond that? It's the Wild West. New coins launch daily. Some are promising. Some are pure hype. Most will vanish. That's why crypto isn't a core investment; it's a speculative layer. You don't build your house on it...but you might wire your house for it just in case.

Used properly, crypto can serve as a diversification play, a hedge against currency debasement, or even a bet on the future of finance. But it can also drain your wealth faster than a rug pull on launch day. That's why this space demands education, caution, and a plan, not just FOMO and memes.

Purpose: Crypto offers upside that few other assets can match, but it comes with high risk and high volatility. It's not a foundational asset class. It's an optional, speculative layer that can amplify gains or losses. For the right investor, a small allocation can add diversification, innovation exposure, and potential long-term asymmetric rewards.

CIO Quick Take: Crypto is like deep-frying a turkey: done right, it can make a delicious Thanksgiving dinner, but if handled carelessly, it can burn down your house. As CIO, you don't ignore it, but you don't go all in either. Start small. Study hard. And only invest what you can afford to lose. If you don't understand the tech, you're not investing, you're gambling.

Chapter Sixteen

Understanding Investment Costs, Fees & Expense Ratios

A s the CIO of You, Inc., you need to be aware of and try to minimize fees as much as possible. Fees and taxes are the silent thieves of the investment world. If you want your dollars to work overtime, you have to know where the leaks are and plug them quickly.

Types of Fees: The Fine Print That Matters

Every investment comes with a price tag. Here are the big three to keep your eye on:

- **Expense Ratios:** This is the annual price you pay for owning a fund, which covers everything from management to paperwork. Low-fee index funds can cost you less than a cup of coffee each year for every $1,000 invested. High-fee funds? They'll eat your lunch.

- **Commissions:** These are the charges for buying or selling investments. Most online brokers have gone commission-free for stocks and ETFs, but always check before you click "buy."

- **Advisory Fees:** If you hire a pro to steer your ship, expect to pay for it, either a flat fee or a cut of your assets. Make sure you're getting real value for the price.

The True Cost of Fees: A Case Study

The fewer fees you pay, the more "employees" (dollars) you have working towards your future. Don't fall for the myth that higher fees mean higher returns. Here's the truth from various sources:

- Less than 3 in 10 actively managed funds beat their passive peers over the last decade.

- Most active funds (57%) underperformed their sector average in the last five years.

- After taxes, 97% of all large- and mid-cap active funds performed worse than index funds.

- Research from the Wharton School of Business found that active fund managers usually don't pick enough winning investments to make up for their higher fees.

Fees may look small, but they're silent thieves of compounding growth. Most investors never notice because the percentage looks harmless, but over time, that little number grows into a big drag on your wealth. Even 1% can quietly rob decades of growth.

For instance, on a **$100,000** investment over **30 years** at **7%**, the investor paying **1%** in fees loses over **$167,000** to costs. Let's make this number more relatable by looking at the stories of High-Fee Henry and Low-Fee Lisa.

High-Fee Henry and Low-Fee Lisa each invest **$250 a month for 30 years**, earning an average of 7% annually. High-Fee Henry invests in actively managed mutual funds with **1% in annual fees.** Low-Fee Lisa invests in low-cost index funds charging **0.05%.** When they both retire, High-Fee Henry ends up with roughly **$245,000**, while Low-Fee Lisa finishes with about **$300,000.**

Same discipline. Same market. Same time frame. The only difference? Fees. High-Fee Henry's extra cost didn't buy better performance, it just bought him less of his own wealth.

Compounding doesn't care who it works for: you or your fees. Every percentage point you save is a raise for your future self. Always know what you're paying, because **invisible fees make invisible thieves.**

CIO Quick Take: Keep it simple. Cut costs. Let broad index funds and ETFs do the heavy lifting for your future.

Final Take: Investment Cost Considerations
Here's the real talk, CIO: Every dollar you save on fees and taxes is a dollar that keeps working for you year after year. The true thieves of the investing world aren't market crashes, company underperformance, or bad headlines; they're the hidden costs and overlooked fees that quietly eat away at your future wealth. The

data doesn't lie: low-cost, broad index funds and ETFs consistently outperform most high-fee, actively managed funds, especially after taxes. Don't let slick marketing or fancy fund names distract you from what really matters: keeping more of your money in your investments.

> **CIO Insight:** Use tax-advantaged accounts to turbocharge your growth and always know where your money is going. Plug the leaks, dodge the silent thieves, and let your investments hustle for you.
> That's how you build wealth with confidence and clarity. That's how you lead as the CIO of You, Inc.

Chapter Seventeen

Tax-Advantaged Accounts: Your Secret Weapon

Tax-advantaged accounts are like secret weapons when investing because they allow more of your money to work and compound. Here are your main tools:

- 401(k): Offered by employers. Your contributions come out of your paycheck before taxes, lowering your taxable income. Bonus: many employers match your contributions, at a minimum, you should always contribute enough to get the employer match – That's FREE money.

- Roth IRA: Your contributions are made with after-tax dollars, but your withdrawals are tax-free in retirement. Plus, you can pull out your contributions (not earnings) anytime, penalty-free.

- Traditional IRA: Contributions are made with after-tax dollars, but are generally tax deductible. Get a tax break now, pay taxes when you withdraw in retirement. Good if you expect to be in a lower tax bracket later.

- Backdoor Roth IRA: If your income is too high to contribute to a Roth IRA directly, you can use a backdoor Roth IRA. This involves contributing to a Traditional IRA and then converting it to a Roth IRA.

- Other IRAs: SEP, SIMPLE, Rollover, and more—each with its own quirks. Choose what fits your situation.

CIO Move
Start with your employer's matching retirement plan (typically 401(k)), then max out a Roth or Traditional IRA based on your tax outlook.

Chapter Eighteen

Risk vs. Reward: What Every Smart CIO Understands

Welcome to the investment tightrope.

R isk and reward are the two ends of your investing seesaw. Lean too far on one side and you're out of balance. Every financial move you make involves some trade-off between safety and potential returns. Here's what the wealthy understand. Risk is inevitable…It can't be avoided; it can only be managed. But, if you're going to take on risk, you'd better get paid for it.

What Is Risk Actually?
People say investing is risky, and they're not wrong. But as Warren Buffett famously put it, "Risk comes from not knowing what you're doing." There's a real possibility that you may lose money investing; at the same time, as you have seen, inflation is quietly causing you to lose money in the form of lost purchasing power. Ironically, not investing means you're guaranteed to lose at the game of money.

Here's what is really risky. Saving dollars in a bank earning less than 1%, while inflation steals 2–4% of your purchasing power every year. Real risk is spending every dollar you earn, never planting seeds for tomorrow.

Don't Avoid, Manage Risk
Risk = Uncertainty. It's the possibility that things won't go as planned, that you'll lose money, miss out on growth, or face unexpected changes. As an investor, you contend with a variety of risks:

- Market Risk: Prices go up and down, sometimes wildly.

- Inflation Risk: Your money doesn't grow fast enough and loses value.

- Liquidity Risk: You can't access your money when you need it.

- Interest Rate Risk: Rates go up, and your bond values fall.

- Credit Risk: A company or government fails to repay its debt.

Everything in life has risk, and investing is no different. As Rick Rule famously says: "The biggest risk to each individual investor is conveniently located to the left of their right ear, and to the right of their left ear."

Walking across the street has risks, but you can't avoid crossing the street altogether. You cross it as intelligently as you can by managing the risk: walk in the cross walk, wait for the green walking symbol, look both ways, and move with intention. Today, you don't see crossing the street as risky as you did as a child. Why? Experience and education. That mix allows you to cross the street with reasonable confidence. As you gain more experience and education in investing, you will develop a similar level of confidence and competence.

Understanding Reward
- Reward = Potential Return. The primary reason for investing is to grow your money. When investing, rewards come in three main forms:

- Capital Appreciation: The value of your investment increases.

- Dividends or Interest: Regular income from stocks or bonds.

- Rental Income: Earnings from real estate investments.

How to Think About Risk Like a Pro
1. Learn Before You Leap: If you can't name three things that could go wrong, you don't know enough yet.

2. Diversify: Don't bet the farm. Spread across sectors, asset classes, and strategies.

3. Match Risk to Time Horizon: The longer your timeline, the more risk you can manage.

4. Control Your Emotions: Most mistakes are made in panic, not in peace.

5. Set Limits: Know what you're willing to lose — before you enter the game.

6. Extend Your Investment Timeline:

    a. The longer your money stays invested, the more it can compound.

    b. Time helps smooth out volatility.

    c. It improves your odds of winning the long game.

Diversification: Why and How

Think of diversification as a financial shock absorbers. By spreading your investments across asset types (stocks, bonds, real estate, metals, etc.), industries, and even regions, you reduce the impact of one bad performer.

Portfolio Allocation

If diversification is spreading your eggs across baskets, allocation is deciding how many eggs go in each one. When done right, allocation matches your mix of investments to your risk tolerance, goals, and timeline.

- Younger investors? More stocks for growth.

- Closer to retirement? More income assets and less volatility.

You can use online calculators, such as Smart Asset's Calculator (https://smartasset.com/), to find a solid starting point for your situation.

> CIO Final Take: There's no such thing as a risk-free investment. But there is such a thing as a risk-smart investor. That's your job. Learn the balance. Practice the discipline. And always make sure your money is moving with intention, not emotion.

Chapter Nineteen

Understanding Return on Investment (ROI)

W e've mentioned that every dollar is an employee, and their #1 job is to bring in more employees. That's not just a cute metaphor. Those "new hires" they bring in? That's **Return on Investment (ROI)** in action.

If your dollars are chilling in a low-yield savings account earning 0.01%, they're basically scrolling TikTok on company time. Dead weight. But when they're out working, earning dividends, gaining value, funding businesses, they're building you a wealth army. That's **ROI.**

How To Calculate ROI?
Return on Investment (ROI) measures how much you get back compared to what you put in.

- ROI = (Net Profit / Cost of Investment) x 100

- If you invest $1,000 and it grows to $1,200, your net profit is $200: ($200/$1,000) x 100 = 20% ROI

- Simple, but powerful.

Start Thinking Like A CIO
Making you the CIO isn't about creating a fun metaphor; it's about helping you make the intellectual, emotional and psychological shifts to reframe the role money plays in your life, as well as how you handle money. Instead of asking, "Can I afford this?" start asking:

- Should I buy this?

- What's the potential benefit to my life vs my wealth?

- What's the opportunity cost? What if I invested the money instead?

- Does the real value of buying "X" today outweigh the benefit of investing those dollars?

Let's use a scenario of purchasing a new car:
- You choose your "dream" car over a more economical vehicle because it's only $200 more a month. But what's the ROI on that decision?

- That same $200 invested monthly at 10% over 5 years would total $14,974. However, if you didn't add another dollar to that $14,974 and waited another 20 years, it would grow to $100,700.

- In reality, that $200 decision is a $100,000 decision over 25 years.

- Ask yourself, how different would your retirement be if you just made a few different decisions like this along the way?

ROI isn't just about money. It's about value.

Beyond the Numbers: The ROI You Can't Always Calculate

Now, here's where it gets real. On paper, the math is clear: the $200/month difference between an economy car and a dream car could cost you $100,000 in future investment growth. But that doesn't automatically make the economy car the "right" choice. Why? Because ROI isn't always about dollars. I know, I know, I just showed you the math formula of how to calculate it. Just stick with me!

Sometimes, the return on a decision is emotional, or psychological, or tied to your time, peace, mental bandwidth, or even your sense of identity. That's a real ROI too, it's just harder to measure. As CIO, your job is to start looking at every major decision through multiple ROI lenses:

- What's the financial return on this choice?

- What's the emotional or mental return?

- What's the energy cost or time impact?

- Is this a short-term dopamine hit or a long-term value move?

Here's the trap though, we often justify bad financial decisions using emotional logic that sounds reasonable:

- "I work hard, I deserve this."

- "This will finally make me feel like I've made it."

- "People will respect me more when they see me with this." Or, "Imagine how good I will look when I pull up in this."

That's not R-O-I...That's E-G-O.

All jokes aside, if the ROI is genuinely about joy, utility, alignment, or saving time in a way that fuels your bigger vision, that's valid. But if the motivation is to impress others, avoid discomfort, or fill a temporary void? That's not your CIO talking. That's your insecurity calling the shots. The real question is this:

Is the emotional return you're hoping for worth more than what those dollars could do if they were working for you instead?

And even deeper:

Will Future You thank you for this decision? Or will they be left wondering what could've been?

> **CIO Insight:** The Rule of ROI. ROI is never just about money, but when you're making value-based decisions, ask yourself: "What's the return: financially, emotionally, mentally, and does it align with the life I'm trying to build?"
>
> If it does? Green light. If it doesn't? Hit pause.
>
> *That self-inquiry and pause is the habit that separates reactive spenders from intentional wealth builders.*

Chapter Twenty

Tools

Activity #1: Asset Class Cheat Sheet: *Your Quick Reference to the Major Investing Categories*

T his is your menu, CIO. Each asset class is a tool. You don't need to use them all, but you do need to know what's on the table so you can build a portfolio that actually works for you.

<u>**Stocks (Equities)**</u>
Partial ownership in a company, you're buying a piece of the business.
Risk Level: Moderate to High
Returns: High over time, but volatile short-term
How You Make Money: Asset appreciation and dividends (profit sharing)
Best For: Long-term growth
Key Notes: Index funds and ETFs can give broad exposure with less risk than selecting individual stocks.

Example ETFs:
- VTI – Total U.S. Stock Market (Vanguard)

- VOO – S&P 500 (Vanguard)

- SCHD – Dividend-focused U.S. Stocks (Schwab)

<u>**Bonds (Fixed Income)**</u>
What It Is: Loans to governments or corporations paid back with interest.
Risk Level: Low to Moderate
Returns: Lower than stocks, more stable
How You Make Money: Interest payments and return of principal
Best For: Income, diversification, and stability

Key Notes: Bonds act like the "shock absorbers" of your portfolio. Bonds don't make you rich, but they keep you from going broke.

Example ETFs:
- BND – Total Bond Market (Vanguard)

- AGG – U.S. Aggregate Bond Market (iShares)

- TIP – Treasury Inflation-Protected Securities (iShares)

Real Estate
What It Is: Physical property or real estate investment trusts (REITs)
Risk Level: Moderate
Returns: Rental income and property value appreciation
How You Make Money: Monthly Cash flow and asset appreciation price growth
Best For: Passive income, inflation hedge
Key Notes: Direct ownership can be high-maintenance. REITs offer a more hands-off option.

Example ETFs:
- VNQ – U.S. Real Estate (Vanguard)

- SCHH – U.S. Real Estate (Schwab)

- REET – Global Real Estate (iShares)

Commodities (Gold, Silver, Oil, etc.)
What It Is: Physical goods with value — often used as raw materials
Risk Level: Moderate to High
Returns: Varies with supply & demand, inflation, and market trends
How You Make Money: Price appreciation
Best For: Inflation protection, crisis hedging
Key Notes: Precious metals (like gold & silver) shine brightest when people lose faith in paper money.

Example ETFs:
- GLD – Gold (SPDR)

- SLV – Silver (iShares)

- DBC – Diversified Commodities (Invesco)

Commodities are insurance. You won't get rich here, but they protect what you've built.

CIO Insight: Commodities give you a defensive line in your portfolio, especially when inflation hits or markets wobble. Real assets like gold, silver, and oil don't flinch when the dollar does — they remind you that wealth isn't just digits, it's *value you can hold.*

Cash & Cash Equivalents
What It Is: Savings accounts, CDs, money market funds Risk Level: Very Low
Returns: Low
How You Make Money: Minimal interest
Best For: Emergency funds, short-term goals
Key Notes: Safe — but inflation eats your buying power over time. Don't overstay here.

Examples:
- High-Yield Savings Accounts (Ally, Marcus, etc.)

- Money Market Funds (Fidelity SPAXX, Vanguard VMFXX)

- 3–6 Month U.S. Treasury Bills

Alternative Asset: Crypto
What It Is: Crypto, collectibles, private equity, farmland, art, etc. Risk Level: High to Extremely High
Returns: Potentially high, but unpredictable
How You Make Money: Appreciation and mining
Best For: Speculative plays and diversification
Key Notes: Only invest what you're willing to lose...Education is mandatory here.

Example ETFs & Platforms:
- BITO – Bitcoin Futures ETF (ProShares)

- GBTC – Grayscale Bitcoin Trust

- ARKW – Includes exposure to blockchain/crypto companies

- Crypto Platforms: Coinbase, Swan Bitcoin, Strike

- Crypto is the wild west. Treat it like hot sauce — a little adds flavor. Too much? You get burned.

CIO Insights (Overall): Every asset class has a role. Think of them like different plants in your garden, some grow fast, some slow, some protect the others.
You don't need everything on this list; you need a blend that fits your timeline, temperament, and goals.
Don't chase what's hot. Build what lasts.

Chapter Twenty-One

Risk Tolerance Quiz

How Spicy Is Your Investing Style?

A s CIO of You, Inc., your job isn't to avoid risk; it's to understand it and manage it like a pro. This quiz will help you determine your natural comfort level with volatility, uncertainty, and long-term investing decisions.

Circle the letter that best describes you. Be honest, this isn't about what sounds smart. It's about knowing yourself so you can invest with confidence.

1. Your reaction if the market drops 15% in one month?

A. I panic. Sell, sell, sell!

B. I get anxious, but I wait it out.

C. I stay calm and may even buy more.

D. It's a sale and go shopping, I've been waiting for this.

2. You've lost $5,000 on paper, what do you do?

A. Withdraw my money. I can't afford to lose more.

B. Do nothing: I'm not thrilled, but I know it's temporary.

C. Revisit my plan and stay the course.

D. Reinvest and look for new opportunities. Make it count.

3. What's your investment time horizon?

A. Less than 3 years: I'll need the money soon.

B. 3–5 years: I'm thinking mid-term.

C. 5–10 years: I'm in this for the long haul.

D. 10+ years: I'm planting trees, not picking flowers.

4. When you hear the word "risk," what do you think?

A. Loss

B. Uncertainty

C. Opportunity

D. Leverage

5. Which investing headline would influence you most?

A. "Crash Imminent: Sell Now!"

B. "Economy Uncertain: Experts Advise Caution"

C. "Buy the Dip? Here's What Long-Term Investors Say"

D. "Savvy Investors Double Down During Pullback"

Your Score:
Count how many of each letter you chose:

Mostly A's – Cautious Conservative
You prefer safety and predictability. You're best suited for lower-risk, stable investments like bonds or index funds with high diversification. As CIO: Focus on building confidence, not chasing returns.

Mostly B's – Steady Builder

You understand investing takes time, but you like to play it smart. You're willing to take some risk, but only with a plan in place. As CIO: Balance growth with stability and keep refining your strategy.

Mostly C's – Confident Grower

You accept volatility as part of the game and stay focused on the long term. You're okay with the ups and downs because you trust the process. As CIO: Double down on your systems and keep learning.

Mostly D's – Risk-Ready Strategist

You're bold, informed, and unshaken by short-term noise. You lean into uncertainty when you see value and have the mindset to match. As CIO: Stay humble and strategic. Make sure data, not ego, backs your boldness. The same risk that builds wealth can also erode it if not managed wisely.

Reflection Prompts:

Based on your results, how do you feel about your current portfolio or investing habits?

What changes, if any, would better align your strategy with your true risk tolerance?

STAGE 3

DESIGNING THE GARDEN

STACKERS UNIVERSITY

Stackers University

Chapter Twenty-Two

Introduction: Designing the Garden

Theme: Systems for Sustainable Growth Goal: Build your financial infrastructure and automate wealth-building habits.

S eeds don't grow well in chaos. Systems build freedom because they replace stress with structure. This is the part where strategy meets structure. In Stage 3, we're no longer just talking about what to grow; we're building the system that ensures it grows and continues to grow even when life gets messy. If Stage 2 was about learning what you could plant, Stage 3 is building and laying out your garden to maximize your efforts. This stage involves installing the infrastructure, your financial irrigation system, which keeps your wealth machine humming without constant supervision. You'll learn:

- How to direct your money flow with purpose and clarity

- How to automate savings and investment

- How to choose the right brokerage accounts, retirement vehicles, and platforms

- How to place your first trade, avoid mistakes, and keep costs low

- How to build a tax-efficient foundation that protects long-term growth

Wealth doesn't grow by accident,□
It grows by design.

Chapter Twenty-Three

Build The Infrastructure

Lay the groundwork for a wealth-building system that works even when you're not watching it.

The best gardens don't grow from willpower. They grow from systems. You can have great seeds (investments) and rich soil (your mindset), but without structure, – no garden beds, no rows, no irrigation – weeds creep in and chaos takes over. In wealth-building, your infrastructure is your flow:

- How your money flows in, moves through, and exits your life.

- How you assign every dollar a job before it wanders off.

- How automation turns your best habits into defaults.

It's about turning good intentions into reliable routines, because you don't rise to the level of your goals, you fall to the level of your systems. This is the moment you stop saying, "I'll try to save more" and start saying, "I've built a system that saves automatically." Here's the brutal truth most people miss: You don't need a bigger paycheck; you need a better pipeline (though a bigger paycheck wouldn't hurt!)

Story: The Bridge That Broke
Let me tell you about a student making over $100K...and still broke. Every month, money came in. Every month, it disappeared. This student didn't just have a spending problem. He had a system failure. He kept trying to spend less and budget better, but what he really needed was a money bridge, a structure that guided a portion of his income toward savings and investments before lifestyle creep could steal it.

Once he started building his bridge, a split deposit here, an auto-transfer there – suddenly, his whole system shifted. His quality of life didn't change much, but his bank accounts and investments did. So much so that his efforts yielded more fruit than he could have ever imagined. In just three years, he saved $250,000.

Some will find this hard to believe. I know I did! Thankfully, *I was that student!* I lived it and still find it hard to believe.

> Build the bridge... Direct the flow... And watch your garden grow.

CIO Tool: Infrastructure Planning Grid
Set up the following pieces in a spreadsheet, notebook, or digital tracker:

Component	Your Current Setup	Upgrade Needed?	Notes/Action Plan
Checking Account		Yes / No	
Emergency Savings		Yes / No	Target: 3–6 months of expenses
High-Yield Savings		Yes / No	For short-term goals
Brokerage Account		Yes / No	For long-term investing
Retirement Accounts		Yes / No	401(k), IRA, Roth, etc.
Income Sources		Yes / No	Wages, side hustle, etc.
Automated Savings		Yes / No	Auto-transfers & deposits
Bill Payments		Yes / No	Autopay or scheduled manually?

Reflection Prompt:
Write it down. Make a plan. Eliminate the friction. Infrastructure may not be sexy, but it's what makes freedom real. When your system is dialed in, you start to feel like Yoda, "Do or do not, there is no try." (Should have warned you about a Dad Joke). Regardless, it just works!

What's one friction point in your current system that's costing you peace of mind, and what would it take to fix it?

Chapter Twenty-Four

Money Flow = Water For The Garden

E ver feel like your bank account has an invisible leak that makes your money disappear? Money in. Money out. Money Gone. You're not crazy! You have the wrong money flow. This will be hard to hear and believe right now, but you don't build wealth with income or with more income. You build it with money flow. If your bank account already has leaks, more money just makes the leak bigger and the loss greater. Water flow is what fuels growth in your garden. Money flow is what fuels your personal Wealth Cycle by breaking the Working Poor Cycle (money flow).

> **Belief Flip:**
> Old Belief: "If I just made more money, I'd finally get ahead."
> New Belief: "It's not just about how much I make, it's about how and where my money flows"

Is your flow towards liabilities and expenses or savings and investments?

Cash Flow DOES NOT = Money Flow
When you understand and implement this, your financial life will change dramatically in 6 months. Cash flow focuses on money in and out of your possession. Simply, it's calculated by subtracting your total monthly expenses (outflow) from your total monthly income (inflow); at best it provides a broad snapshot. If cash flow is like taking a picture, money flow is like watching a video, it shows direction, momentum, and purpose. Just because money comes in and out, doesn't mean your money is moving with purpose.

Cash flow is what's left after your lifestyle takes it's bite. Money flow is what gets INTENTIONALLY directed to specific areas of your life. Until you control the flow, your income will continue to leak out of your bank account. Just as in a garden, you must control your watering system (flow) to account for each plant's different water needs.

Sometimes, it's not about more water, but about fixing the direction and flow of your waterlines. This way, increases in water flow don't get wasted away. Money flow is what turns income into freedom, because without it, even six figures will have you living check-to-check. With it, even modest earnings can become a wealth-building engine.

Don't believe that? Do you still believe all your problems would be solved with more income?

Statistics on Living Paycheck to Paycheck by Income

Income Level	% Living Paycheck to Paycheck
Less than $50,000	80%
$50,000 – $99,999	66%
$100,000 – $199,999	51%
$200,000+	33%

You would think that the $100K tipping point would have a significant difference...Nope, only 15%. But WHY? The answer lies in the next two statements I want you to commit to memory, and post on your bathroom mirror:

> **1. It's not about how much you make; it's about how much you spend.**

> **2. No amount of income can solve a spending problem.**

If your money flow is wrong or misdirected, your income could double overnight and the only difference is that you'd have nicer "things," but you'd still be just as broke at the end of the month. That's why so many folks making six figures still feel poor; they've never built a money flow system that actually works. That's why infrastructure matters...It's why automation matters...It's why paying yourself first matters. Fixing your money flow won't guarantee that you will be wealthy, but it will ensure that you won't be poor.

The CIO Mindset: Get Clarity Before Strategy
As CIO of You, Inc., your most important task isn't picking stocks or opening brokerage accounts; it's mastering the flow. You need to know:

- What's coming in (net income)

- What's going out (expenses)

- What's staying in place (savings/investing)

- And what's slipping through the cracks (leaks, lifestyle creep, etc.)

Don't gloss over this. Financial clarity is what separates those who build wealth from those who merely wish for it.

The Flow Formula
Here's a simple 3-part framework for understanding and improving your flow:

1. Track the Inflow

Start with your net income (after taxes and deductions). Don't use gross income; that's fantasy money. We want to know what actually hits your account each month. Common inflows:

- Job income

- Side hustles

- Passive income (dividends, rental, etc.)

- Government benefits or child support

2. Audit the Outflow

Where is your money actually going? Not where you think it's going. Categories to examine:

- Fixed expenses (rent/mortgage, car payment, subscriptions)

- Variable expenses (food, gas, utilities)

- Non-essentials (Amazon runs, DoorDash, retail therapy)

- Debts and minimum payments

Pro tip: Pull the last 90 days of statements and highlight your "leaks," spending that doesn't align with your values or goals.

3. Free the Flow

Once you know your income and expenses, calculate your net cash flow:

Net Cash Flow = Inflow – Outflow

If it's negative or barely positive, you have a problem. Not a personal flaw, just a systems flaw. Your job is to increase the gap between inflow and outflow, and redirect that gap into wealth (savings, debt payoff, investing). Remember the Jim Rohn quote from earlier: *"When your outflow exceeds your income, your upkeep becomes your downfall."*

CIO Insight: Audit Your Workforce Before You Automate
Before you automate anything, pause and do a quick audit of your workforce. Some **employees (dollars)** are loyal and show up for work (savings, investing, debt reduction), others disappear the second they hit your account. Ask yourself: Which of my dollars are actually working for me? Which are ghosting me and costing me wealth?

Automation is powerful, but if you're automating waste, you're not growing a garden - you're watering weeds.

Audit first – then automate with intention.

Reflection Prompt:
What's one unnecessary expense you're willing to cut or reduce this month to free up more cash for your future? Write it down. Then redirect it. That's how the game changes.

Final Word: Don't Just Earn More: Flow Better
You're not trying to work harder forever. You're trying to redirect the flow so your money goes where you desire and works for you. This chapter isn't about restriction; it's about release. Release your money from chaos. Release yourself from confusion by setting up a system where your money flows in alignment with your goals.

Chapter Twenty-Five

Paying Yourself First

Break the Cycle, Redirect the Flow

I f your money disappears every month before it has a chance to build wealth, welcome to the club nobody wants to be in. This chapter is your way out.

The Working Poor Cycle traps millions as displayed below. You earn...you pay taxes...you cover bills...swipe a few cards...buy groceries...buy a few things you can't remember buying, only to count down the days to the next paycheck.

Why? Because your money flow is reactive, not intentional. The first way you break free from this cycle is by paying yourself first. It's your wealth cycle/system that is broken. You work hard. You pay taxes. You cover expenses. And then poof, it's all gone before you know it...No wealth...No margin...No options.

Belief Flip:
Old Belief: "I'll save whatever's left over at the end of the month."
New Belief: "I pay myself first, because I'm the most important bill."

Money Flow Must Be Intentional

You don't build wealth with leftovers. You build it by directing your money flow, ensuring it moves with intention before anyone else gets a piece. That's what "pay yourself first" is all about. This is about prioritizing, not budgeting. This is you saying, "Before I give a dollar to my landlord, lender, or lifestyle, I'm investing in me first." When you make YOU, your first bill, your savings grow automatically, your investments get funded, and your superpower (time) is activated, allowing wealth to start compounding, what Einstein called the 8th Wonder of the World.

Think back to the Breaking the Working Poor Cycle graphic: Right after income, the cycle should move to savings, not to spending. This single pivot reroutes your money flow and is the first step in building a **Wealth Cycle**.

You go from:

Work → Taxes → Bills → Lifestyle → Zero Left
To

Work → Savings/Investing → Bills → Lifestyle → Freedom

This is money flow mastery in action. Now, notice the new flow that happens when you change just one thing: paying yourself first.

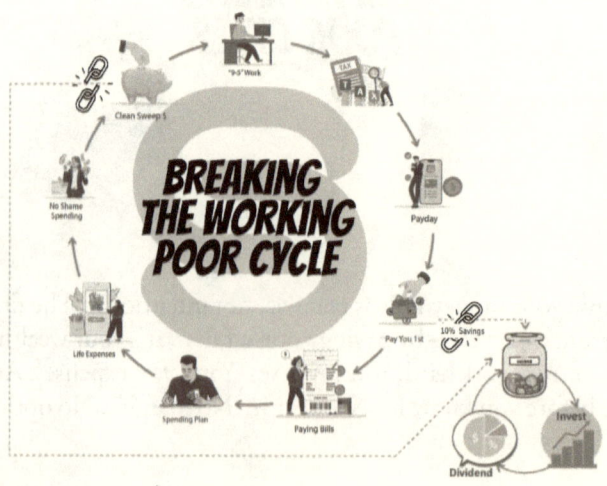

That's it. That's the shift. You planted seeds to break the cycle, and that small trickle will become a river as you build wealth.

Why This Is So Critical
- You treat saving and investing like non-negotiable bills, not afterthoughts.

- You lock in progress before life gets in the way.

- You stop waiting for motivation and start building momentum.

Growing wealth is not about lack or living a life of lack; it's about being intentional. You can enjoy what your heart desires, without overspending, AFTER you pay yourself first. Most people match their spending to the money sitting in their account, which is why paying yourself first matters so much. It sets financial boundaries automatically. But here's the best part; once you've paid yourself and paid your bills, what's left is what I call **"No Shame Spending."** You earned it. You handled business. Go enjoy your life and spend without guilt. Want that $500 purse? Grab it, as long as it comes from your No Shame Spending allocation.

Finally, let's quickly discussed the "**Clean Sweep icon.**" It's the final move that clears your leftover employees (dollars) and keeps them from sneaking back into spending. We'll unpack in fully in the *Creating Your Wealth Cycle* chapter, for now, remember this: **don't leave idle money in your checking account where temptation lives.**

CIO Insight: Mindset Shift...You Are the Priority
As CIO of You, Inc., you're not just a bill-payer. You're a wealth-builder. That means creating a system where your money flows to your future first. If you don't pay close attention to your employees, they will flow to someone who does.

Reflection Prompt (Write it Down)
What would change in your financial life if your savings and investing were handled before your bills, not after? What would that freedom feel like?

Final Word: Break the Cycle, Rewire the Flow.
Paying yourself first is a strategy and a statement. It says:

> I matter... My future matters... My employees (money) matter... My employees are treated like they matter... And I'm building my wealth, not someone else's.

The wealthy don't wait to save what's left. They save first, spend second. Now, you do too! Break the cycle, redirect the flow, and fund your freedom.

Chapter Twenty-Six

Automate Your Wealth Cycle

Lock in the Wins. Elevate the Flow.

Y ou've built the bridge. You've redirected the flow. Now it's time to automate the process, because systems don't rely on willpower. They rely on wiring. The most powerful wealth cycles aren't built on hustle. They're built on habits that happen automatically. Automation protects your best intentions from your worst impulses. #FACTS. The goal is to move from reactive spender to proactive investor, by default.

Wealth Cycle Money Flow

Earlier, we introduced the concept of Breaking the Working Poor Cycle as a way to establish your personal ecosystem for managing money flow. Every cycle starts with you working→ getting taxed → receiving your paycheck. The first bridge we built was the "Pay Yourself First" off-ramp, where at least 10% of your income flowed straight into savings and investments. Now, we're reinforcing that bridge and every other good habit, with automation. You need to ensure that each dollar that enters your ecosystem automatically flows where it's supposed to go, without thought, effort, or delay.

> **Belief Flip:**
> Old Belief: "If I just try harder, I'll finally get ahead."
> New Belief: "I don't need more effort; I need better systems."

Systems...Save

Systems save you in almost every aspect. They help you save time, energy, effort, and prevent mental fatigue. You're trying to juggle multiple due dates, manually transferring money, calculating "safe to spend" amounts, while trying to stay motivated, which is a recipe for disaster. In fact, it's a trap. Here's how you escape:

1. **Build Systems:** We've covered this enough...They lower brain load and make wealth-building automatic.

2. **Use Automatic Pay:** Stop relying on memory, motivation, or mood

to pay your bills. Set up automatic payments for fixed expenses, such as rent, car payments, utilities, and minimum debt payments. This ensures nothing gets missed, avoids late fees, and protects your credit. Automation is protection; it's not just convenience, it's part of your wealth defense system. When your brain isn't cluttered with due dates, you have more mental bandwidth to focus on building, not just surviving.

3. **Use the Clean Sweep Method:** After each turn of your wealth cycle, you want to utilize the Clean Sweep Method. Ideally, before your next paycheck is deposited, you move any unspent "leftover" funds. You sweep leftover funds into your savings before your next paycheck hits. You've proven you don't need to spend every dollar in your budget; now, bank those bonus funds into your savings.

A Word of Caution: automation doesn't mean you stop paying attention. Set aside time each month to review your accounts, confirm payments, and check for false charges or forgotten subscriptions that quietly drain your wealth. Automation should free your mind, not blind your awareness. It gives you space to think strategically, but *you* still need to monitor and manage the system.

Elevate: Go Beyond Automation
Set it and forget it? Nah. Set it. Review it. Upgrade it.

Strategy	Description
Annual Raise Rule	Every raise means increasing your saving/investing percentage before upgrading lifestyle
Calendar Reviews	Quarterly check-in to realign with evolving goals
Micro-Investing	Apps that invest spare change automatically
Windfall Rule	Bonuses, refunds, or gifts? Default: 50% invest, 25% save, 25% enjoy
Lifestyle Cap	Cap lifestyle spending to ensure future income flows toward wealth

Reflection Prompt:
- Where is your current system causing friction or stress?

- What's one tweak you can make this week to reduce that burden? Write it down. Then do it.

Final Word: Systems Are the Silent Superpower
Your system isn't just about efficiency, it's about freedom.
It frees your time.
It frees your energy.
It frees your money from chaos.

Wealthy people don't ask, "Did I remember to save this month?" Their system already did it for them. So set it. Forget it. Review it. Upgrade it. Upgrade it when life changes and let your system grow your future, one automated move at a time. Let's systemize your success, so wealth becomes your new normal.

Chapter Twenty-Seven

The Planting Guide

How To Choose Investments That Match Your System

This chapter is designed to help you choose simple, effective investments that align with your goals, temperament, and timeline, without getting overwhelmed by hype, complexity, or decision fatigue.

Let's keep it all the way real: For over 90% of people, a well-diversified mix of low-cost ETFs is all you'll ever need. It's not sexy...It's not clickbait...But it works. The financial media, the Wall Street Bros and social media influencers will try to convince you that "real investors" pick individual stocks or time the market. But the data tells a different story; most actively managed funds underperform basic index funds. Period. And that's before we even factor in the fees. In fact, let's dig into fees.

- Let's say you invest $100,000 for 30 years with an average return of 8%.

- With a low-cost ETF charging 0.5%, you'd end up with around $758,000

- With a managed fund charging 1.5%, you'd walk away with closer to $574,000

That's nearly $184,000 lost to fees... Same market... Same returns... Just more skimming. You don't need to outperform Wall Street. You just need your money in the market, invested consistently, with low fees, in alignment with your personal wealth cycle. That's the game.

Now, is there a place for individual stocks or more advanced strategies? Absolutely, but for beginners, or anyone looking to build long-term wealth with minimal effort, ETFs are the path to wealth. Remember, your priority is to get invested and stay invested in proven vehicles that compound over time.

Most importantly, this guide is not here to tell you what to buy; it's to help you understand the various categories so you can build a portfolio that matches your values and vision.

ETF tickers and Summaries

You ever scroll past a ticker like VTI or QQQ and think, "That's just Wall Street gibberish"? Learning to read an ETF ticker and summary is like learning to read a nutrition label. You don't need to memorize everything; you just need to know what matters. Let's break it down.

What's in a Ticker?

A stock or ETF's ticker is its nickname on the stock market. It's how you find and buy it, for example, "AAPL" pulls up Apple. Here are a few tickers you might see:

- VTI – Vanguard Total Stock Market

- SPY – SPDR S&P 500 ETF

- QQQ – Invesco Nasdaq-100

- SCHD – Schwab U.S. Dividend Equity

Quick Decode:
The letters don't always stand for something directly.
But once you get familiar with a few tickers, you'll recognize what they track and who manages them (Vanguard, Schwab, iShares, etc.).

ETF Research Tools That Make It Make Sense

If you want a clean summary of everything below (and more), sites like ETF.com and Morningstar.com offer free profiles with performance, holdings, risks, and comparisons. They're great for digging deeper without drowning in jargon.

CIO Insight: You don't need to become an ETF encyclopedia. You do need to know how to vet what you're buying. When you buy an ETF, you're buying a basket of businesses, a strategy, and a cost structure. Read the label before you invest.

Core ETF categories

As shared previously, you don't need a thousand tickers or a finance degree to build a strong portfolio. What you do need is clarity on the handful of ETF categories that form the foundation of most long-term investing strategies.

Think of these categories as your garden's core crops or the foundational investments that should make up the bulk of your investments. From there, you can add specialty plants later (sector funds, international plays, etc.), but only after you've planted the staples. Regardless of the broker you use, all have some version of the ETF categories outlined below. A more comprehensive list is available in Appendix B.

1. S&P 500 ETFs: The Bread and Butter of U.S. Investing
Tracks the S&P 500, the 500 largest publicly traded U.S. companies (think Apple, Microsoft, Amazon, Google, etc.). It's a quick way to own a slice of the biggest, most established names in the market. These funds instantly diversify you across hundreds of companies with just one fund. Historically, the S&P 500 has delivered 7–10% average annualized returns over the long term. This is a classic "set it and let it grow" option.

Popular Examples:

- VOO (Vanguard)

- SPY (State Street)

- IVV (iShares)

CIO Quick Take: If you only ever owned one ETF, this wouldn't be a bad choice. It's not flashy, but it's proven.

2. Total U.S. Market ETFs: Everything, Everywhere, All at Once
These funds hold every publicly traded U.S. stock (big, mid, small, and micro-cap). More exposure than just the S&P 500, this gives you growth potential from smaller companies and startups that aren't in the S&P yet.

Popular Examples:

- VTI (Vanguard Total Stock Market)

- SCHB (Schwab)

- ITOT (iShares)

CIO Quick Take: If S&P 500 is the MVP, this is the entire starting lineup...A little more volatile, but a little more growth potential too.

3. Dividend ETFs: The Paycheck Players

These dividend-paying companies are especially useful for folks nearing retirement, or those who want "income while they wait" for capital growth.

Popular Examples:

- VYM (Vanguard High Dividend Yield)

- SCHD (Schwab Dividend Equity)

- DVY (iShares Select Dividend)

CIO Quick Take: These ETFs let you plant a tree that drops fruit every quarter.

4. Growth ETFs: The Rocket Fuel (With a Seatbelt)

These focus on fast-growing companies that reinvest profits into expansion instead of paying dividends. Think tech and innovation. The higher potential upside does come with more volatility and risk. Great for younger investors or folks with a longer time horizon.

Popular Examples:

- VUG (Vanguard Growth)

- QQQ (Invesco Nasdaq 100)

- IWF (iShares Russell 1000 Growth)

CIO Quick Take: Lots of action, just make sure it's a piece of your portfolio, not the whole thing.

5. Bond ETFs: The Stabilizers

Typically, they offer lower returns but more stability. When stocks dip, bonds can help cushion the blow. Ideal for conservative investors or for rebalancing in retirement.

Popular Examples:

- BND (Vanguard Total Bond Market)

- AGG (iShares Core U.S. Aggregate Bond)

- TLT (iShares 20+ Year Treasury Bond)

CIO Quick Take: You don't get rich on bonds, but they're the shock absorbers of your portfolio. Use them for balance, not for glory.

You've done the work most people avoid. You've now built the foundation most people spend a lifetime avoiding. From this point forward, your system works even when you don't. That's how freedom grows and wealth is generated.

Chapter Twenty-Eight

Tools

Account Type Quick Reference Sheet

Account Type	Best For	Tax Benefits	Contribution Limits (2025)	Access Rules	Common Platforms
Taxable Brokerage	Flexibility & long-term wealth	No upfront tax benefit, but long-term capital gains are taxed lower than income	No limit	Withdraw anytime (but may owe taxes on gains)	Fidelity, Schwab, Vanguard, Public, Robinhood
Roth IRA	Tax-free growth & retirement	Pay taxes now, grow tax-free, no taxes on withdrawals in retirement	$7,000/year ($8,000 if 50+) — income limits apply	Withdraw contributions anytime; earnings penalty-free at age 59½ (or earlier for qualified reasons)	Fidelity, Schwab, Vanguard, M1 Finance
Traditional IRA	Tax deduction now & retirement	Contribute pre-tax, grows tax-deferred, pay taxes when you withdraw	$7,000/year ($8,000 if 50+) — income phaseouts apply if you have a 401(k)	Withdraw penalty-free at 59½; taxes owed on withdrawals	Fidelity, Schwab, Vanguard
401(k) or 403(b)	Employer retirement plan	Contributions lower taxable income; grows tax-deferred	$23,000/year ($30,500 if 50+)	Withdraw penalty-free at 59½; early withdrawals may have penalties	Through your job/employer
Roth 401(k)	Higher contribution limits + tax-free retirement	Pay taxes now, grow tax-free, no taxes in retirement	$23,000/year ($30,500 if 50+)	Same rules as traditional 401(k)	Through your job (if offered)
HSA (Health Savings Account)	Triple tax benefits (for health + investing)	Tax-deductible in, grows tax-free, tax-free if used for medical	$4,150 (individual) / $8,300 (family)	Can invest funds after balance grows; penalty for non-medical use before age 65	Lively, Fidelity, HSA Bank, employer plans

CIO Insights:

- Taxable accounts = flexibility. Use these for wealth building outside of retirement.

- Roth = tax-free later. Perfect for young investors expecting to grow their income.

- Traditional = tax break now. Ideal if you're in a high tax bracket today.

- 401(k)/IRA = foundational. Start here if your job offers a match, it's free money.

- HSA = secret weapon. If eligible, it's one of the most tax-efficient accounts in existence.

Platform Comparison Chart

Choose the Right Tool for Your Wealth-Building System.

Platform	Best For	Fees	Auto-Investing	Standout Features	Watch For...
Fidelity	Long-term investors who want reliability and full control	$0 commissions on stocks/ETFs	✅ Yes	Highly trusted, great customer service, solid research tools, HSA integration	Clunky mobile app UI (improving), may feel overwhelming to total beginners
Vanguard	Retirement savers & index fund purists	$0 for Vanguard ETFs, some fees for outside funds	✕ Not native, but you can schedule recurring transfers	Ownership model (clients = shareholders), rock-solid reputation	Website feels dated; not ideal for frequent changes or younger UX
Charles Schwab	Balanced platform for both all investors	$0 commissions	✅ Yes	Sleek app, strong support, great ETF selection	Less "hip," some find the interface bland
M1 Finance	Automation nerds who want to "set it and forget it"	$0 trades	✅ Yes — it's the whole model	"Pies" make portfolio building visual and easy; great for DCA	No real-time trading (1–2 windows/day); not ideal for active traders
Public	Beginner-friendly with social investing vibes	$0 commissions	✅ Yes (recurring buys)	Easy UI, educational overlays, ability to follow other investors	Limited analytics, more of a learning tool than a long-term home base
Robinhood	Simplicity and fast trades	$0 trades	✅ Yes	Super simple to use, instant deposits, fast execution	Reputation concerns, gamification tactics, limited investor education
SoFi Invest	New investors who want a "starter pack"	$0 trades	✅ Yes	Combines investing with banking, loans, and financial planning	Limited fund options; more lifestyle app than serious brokerage

CIO Insights:

- **No platform is perfect.** Choose based on your stage, personality, and system.

- **Avoid shiny apps** if they distract you from the long game.

- **You can open more than one account** — just stay organized.

- **Your behavior matters more than your brokerage.** Automate wisely and stay consistent.

ETF & Index Fund Cheat Sheet

Use this as a quick reference to choose investments that match your system and stage.

Fund Type	What It Tracks	Why It Matters	Common Examples	When to Use
Total Market Fund	Entire U.S. stock market (large, mid, and small-cap companies)	Broad exposure, great for beginners, captures overall growth of U.S. economy	VTI (Vanguard), ITOT (iShares), FZROX (Fidelity)	When you want to keep it simple and diversified in one fund
S&P 500 Index Fund	Top 500 U.S. companies by market cap	Focused on large, stable companies, historical backbone of investing	SPY (ETF), VOO (Vanguard), FXAIX (Fidelity index fund)	When you want big-name exposure with lower volatility
Dividend ETF	Stocks that regularly pay dividends	Generates passive income with capital growth possible	VYM (Vanguard), SCHD (Schwab), DVY (iShares)	For income in retirement or to reinvest dividends
Bond ETF	U.S. government or corporate bonds	Adds stability, reduces risk, buffers stock market dips	BND (Total Bond), AGG (iShares Core), TLT (Long-term Treasury)	To balance risk or create a safer income stream
International ETF	Developed or emerging markets outside the U.S.	Adds global diversification, potential growth in rising economies	VXUS (Vanguard Total Intl), VEU (All-World ex-US), IEMG (Emerging Markets)	When you want exposure to global markets
Thematic/ Sector ETF	Specific industries (tech, energy, real estate, etc.)	Targeted bets on sectors you believe in or want to overweight	XLK (Tech), XLE (Energy), VNQ (Real Estate)	When you want to express a strong view or tilt your portfolio
Target Date Fund	Adjusts allocation based on retirement year	"Set it and forget it" option. Auto-adjusts from growth to safety	VTTSX (Vanguard 2060), FDEWX (Fidelity 2055)	When you want one fund that evolves with you

CIO Insights:
- You don't need to own *all* of these; you only need what fits your personal system and timeline.

- Simpler is often better. Master a few building blocks before you chase complexity.

- Your job isn't to find the "perfect" fund, it's to **stay consistent and stay invested.**

Chapter Twenty-Nine

Step-by-Step Trade Practice Guide

How to Buy Your First ETF — CIO Style (Fidelity Edition)

W hy This Matters

This isn't just about making your first trade; it's about stepping into your role as Chief Investment Officer (CIO) of your financial life. Buying an ETF might feel intimidating at first, but once you do it, you'll realize it's just a system. And the sooner you master the system, the sooner you can automate your future wealth. This guide walks you through placing your first ETF order, using Fidelity as the example, with clear steps you can follow on the web or mobile.

Before You Begin: What You Need
- A funded Fidelity brokerage account (not an IRA unless you're investing specifically for retirement)

- A ticker symbol (e.g.):

  ○ VTI = Total U.S. Market

  ○ VOO = S&P 500

  ○ ITOT = iShares Total Market

- A small amount of money to start with (even $25–$100 is fine)

The 6-Step Process

Step 1: Log In to Fidelity

- Visit fidelity.com or open the Fidelity app

- Use your username/password to access your account dashboard

Step 2: Navigate to Trade
- On the main menu, click "Accounts & Trade"

- Select "Trade" or go to the Trading Dashboard

- Choose the correct Brokerage account

Step 3: Find Your ETF
- In the "Trade" window, enter the ticker symbol (e.g., VTI)

- Verify that the ETF name and price match what you expected

Step 4: Place Your Order
- Action: Select Buy

- Quantity Type: Choose Dollars (fractional shares) or Shares (whole)

- Amount: Enter how much you want to invest (e.g., $50)

- Order Type: Select Market Order (executes at current price)

- Timing: Use "Day" unless you're placing a limit order

Don't overthink it. Start with a market order. The goal here is reps, not perfection.

Step 5: Preview & Submit
- Click Preview Order

- Double-check the ETF, account, and amount

- Click Place Order to complete your trade

Congrats, you just became an investor.

Step 6: Review and Track
- Click Activity & Orders to confirm the trade was placed

- You'll see:

  ○ Filled – completed

  ○ Pending – waiting for the market to open

  ○ Canceled – didn't go through

CIO Insight: Every trade is a vote for your future. This isn't about chasing gains; it's about building a habit.
- You're training yourself to invest consistently

- You're learning to trust your system

- You're building muscle memory that separates passive spectators from real stackers

---

Bonus Practice: Set Up Recurring Investments
Fidelity allows you to auto-invest in ETFs weekly, bi-weekly, or monthly. To set it up:

- Go to the ETF's page

- Click Set Up Auto Investing

- Choose your amount and schedule

Even $25/month can turn into tens of thousands over time. The habit is more important than the amount.

STAGE 4

WEATHERING THE SEASONS

STACKERS UNIVERSITY

Stackers University

Chapter Thirty

Introduction: Weathering the Seasons

Theme: Mental Discipline & Emotional Resilience
Goal: Stay grounded through market cycles by understanding your emotions and trusting your strategy

Let's keep it real: Every investor faces a season that tests their faith – when logic clashes with fear and patience feels impossible. The market doesn't just test your money; it tests your mindset. There are entire books on fear, risk, and investor behavior, but you don't need to master them all today. Your job right now is simple: start investing, keep investing, and learn to manage your emotions just enough not to sabotage your own growth. The rest will come with time.

Markets rise and fall. News cycles spin fear. Emotions run wild. Most people don't lose money because of bad investments, they lose it because of bad reactions.

This stage is about building your resilience. You'll learn how to stay grounded when fear creeps in, recognize emotional traps like greed and panic, and stick to your plan when everything in you wants to pull out.

Just like a gardener prepares for droughts, floods, and unexpected weather, you'll learn how to protect both your financial garden and your peace of mind.

It's not just about what you invest in, it's about who you become in the process.

Chapter Thirty-One

"Weather"-Proof Your Mindset

Prepare for Market Storms Before They Hit

If you think investing should always feel safe, you're not investing, you're hiding. It's not meant to feel steady or predictable either, markets move because people do. And if you're chasing calm or comfort, you'll never build conviction. The market doesn't move in straight lines, and your emotions won't either. But long-term investors don't get rich avoiding the rain; they build protective covers, plant deep roots, and keep showing up through every season.

This chapter is about anchoring your mind, not timing the market. Because storms are coming, and if you can't stay grounded, you'll get swept away. Most people don't lose money because of a bad stock pick; they lose because of bad reactions to the market...They panic during dips, chase during booms, or freeze during uncertainty. If you want to build real wealth, your mindset is the first thing that needs armor. *Market drops are inevitable; your reaction is optional.*

Belief Flip:
Old Belief: "Good investors avoid losses."
New Belief: "Good investors expect losses and keep going anyway."

The Garden Metaphor: Droughts, Floods & Seasons

All gardeners know that there are seasons and conditions that are outside of their control. The same is true when investing. For example:

- Droughts = Market crashes

- Floods = Excess hype, speculation

- Frost = Economic downturns

- Pests = Emotional triggers & bad advice

- Weeds = Lifestyle creep and debt

Just like nature, markets have their own rhythm: droughts, floods, and seasons that don't ask for your permission. But your seeds will still grow, as long as you stay resilient and keep showing up through every cycle.

The Market Rewards Resilience
Let's talk facts:

- **Stock market:** Over the last 100 years, despite wars, recessions, and political chaos, the U.S. stock market has still returned 7–10% annually after inflation."

- **Real estate:** Historically returns 4–6% annually plus rental income potential.

- **Long-term investors win:** If you missed just 10 of the best days in the S&P 500 over the past 20 years, your returns would be cut in half.

CIO Insight: Stay Anchored
- Build a plan that works in all weather.

- Set up automation so panic doesn't get a vote.

- Anchor before the storm hits, not during it.

Reflection Prompt
What was your first emotional reaction to a financial storm, such as a dip, a bad news headline, or a crash? What would your future self say to you in that moment?

Final Word: Calm
Smart investing isn't about always knowing what to do, especially during financial storms. It is about not doing something dumb when you feel emotional. Calm investors compound, stay in the market and weather the storms. Mentally prepare yourself now, so when the skies darken, you don't flinch, you keep tending to your garden.

Chapter Thirty-Two

Outsmarting Your Emotions

Master the Internal Game of Investing

You already know the market is going to test you. But here's what nobody tells you: it's not the market that ruins most portfolios, it's you, the investor. Fear, greed, panic, and mental overload sabotage more wealth than any recession ever could. That means your real opponent isn't Wall Street, it is the emotional wiring to the left of your right ear and to the right of your left ear.

This chapter gives you the tools to fight back. To catch your emotional triggers before they hijack your plan. To think in the presence of your emotions, rather than being driven by them. Thinking and emotions work like a see-saw. When one is high, the other is often low. If you don't learn to manage your emotions, your emotions will manage your money.

You can have the best strategy in the world, but if you fold every time the market shakes, your system won't matter. Successful investing is about discipline and emotional control. The best investors aren't fearless; they act in the presence of their fear, which is called courage.

Belief Flip:
Old Belief: "I make financial decisions based on logic."
New Belief: "If I don't manage my emotions, my emotions will manage my money."
The key is to think in the presence of your emotions, not with them.

The Big 3 Triggers (and How to Spot Them)
1. Fear
The moment the market dips or the news goes red, fear whispers: "You're gonna lose everything. Pull out. Protect yourself." Fear convinces you that a short-term loss is the end of the road.

2. Greed
This shows up during bull runs or hype cycles and makes you believe: "If I don't buy now, I'll miss out!" Greed leads to chasing prices, gains and trends. It makes you abandon your plan and buy at a higher price.

Solution: Stick to your allocation and your game plan. Someone winning in another area doesn't mean you're losing. Play your game and never let FOMO dictate your decisions.

3. Recency Bias
This one feels logical: "This dip is different." "That stock always goes up." It tricks you into overestimating recent events and underestimating long-term patterns. For example, after 2008, millions stayed out of the market for years, missing a record-breaking recovery.

Solution: Learn from the past. Don't relive it. Let data, not headlines, guide you.

CIO Insight: Strategy
Build an Emotional Firewall by Relying on Your Systems. Set up your firewall:

- Pre-commit to your plan. Decide now how you'll respond to dips, gains, and noise.

- Automate your contributions. Emotion doesn't get a vote if your system runs the money.

- Write your "calm statement." One sentence you'll read when fear hits.

Example: "I built this plan for the next 10 years, and overall, the stock market provides a 10% return. 'Blank Event' isn't going to ruin my plan."

Quick Facts:
- 91% of individual investors underperform the market, not because of bad investments, but because of a lack of control and trying to time the markets.

- Most buy high (greed) and sell low (fear).

- The market average beats most humans not because it's smarter, but because it's consistent.

- Fidelity executive David Ricciardelli noted: "The accounts with the best returns belong to people who had died or had forgotten they had accounts."

- The simplest and most powerful investing strategy? Stay calm... Sit tight... Let your money grow. The best investors aren't always active; they are patient because they control their emotions.

Reflection Prompt

Which of the three triggers (Fear, Greed, Recency Bias) hits you hardest? When did it last affect one of your financial decisions? What system, script, or reminder can you use to stop it next time?

Final Word: Your Mind is the Market

The financial battlefield isn't "out there," it's in your head. Once you start winning there, your money will follow. Let this chapter serve as your mirror and shield, helping you see yourself clearly. You've got this, CIO! Stay focused on your systems and strategy.

Chapter Thirty-Three

Tools

Activity #1: Market Crash Checklist
What to Do When the Market Tanks (Without Losing Your Mind)

First, Remember Your Role: You're not a panicked investor; you're the CIO of your life. You respond with strategy, not react with emotions.

Step 1: Pause. Breathe. Zoom Out.
- Check your time horizon. Are you investing for retirement 15–30 years from now? If so, this dip is just noise.

- Pull up your plan or portfolio notes. What was your original strategy?

- Has anything about your goals changed? If not, stay the course.

- Avoid doomscrolling. Turn off news/social media; the loudest voices are rarely the wisest during chaos.

Step 2: Evaluate Your System
- Is your emergency fund intact? If yes, you don't need to touch investments. If no, consider pausing new contributions and replenishing cash first.

- Are you properly diversified? Do you have all your money in one stock? or sector?

- Rebalancing after recovery may be wise.

- Do you have recurring investments set up? Down markets = discounted shares. Let your system buy low while everyone else panics.

Step 3: Audit Your Emotions
- Name what you're feeling: Fear? Regret? Panic? Write it down.

- Ask: "What would my CIO self do right now?" Not the scared version of you. The future-focused, data-driven you.

- Talk to someone you trust (not someone who's freaking out too).

- Calm voices create clarity.

Step 4: Take Constructive Action
- Re-read your long-term goals. This crash doesn't change your mission; it tests your commitment to it.

- Consider buying more (only if your foundation is solid).

- Crashes create opportunity. Just make sure your house is in order before adding fuel.

- Celebrate your discipline. You stayed calm. You stayed strategic. You're building emotional wealth too.

> *"Volatility is the price of admission, and*
> *wealth is the reward for staying in your seat."*

Activity #2: Outsmarting Your Emotions
Emotional Audit Worksheet for the CIO-In-Training

Why This Matters
Your emotions are real, but they're not always right. As the CIO, you don't suppress your feelings; you interrogate them. You learn to think in the presence of your emotions, not with your emotions. This worksheet is your self-check system. Use it anytime you feel:

- Panic during market dips

- FOMO when something's pumping

- Guilt about past money mistakes

- Impulse to spend or sell

- Pressure to "do something" without clarity

Emotional Audit Prompts
1. What am I feeling right now?
   - Fear

   - Excitement

   - Regret

   - FOMO

   - Shame

   - Frustration

   - Anxiety

   - Something else:

2. What triggered this emotion? (Example: "Saw the market drop 3%,")

3. Is this feeling tied to a pattern or a one-time event?
   - Pattern I've noticed before

   - One-time situation

- Not sure yet

4. What story am I telling myself right now? (Example: "I should have known better.")

5. Pause + Pivot: What would my CIO self do?
   - Stick to the plan

   - Zoom out to the 5 or 10-year view

   - Talk to someone wise before reacting

   - Revisit my values & goals

   - Journal instead of taking action

   - Other:

6. What action (if any) should I take after the emotion has passed?

Final Reflection
"Feelings are data, not directives. I lead with wisdom, not reaction. I'm the CIO of my future."

STAGE 5

THE FRUIT-BEARING TREE

Stackers University

Chapter Thirty-Four

Introduction: The Fruit-Bearing Tree

Theme: Scale, Legacy & Wealth with Purpose Goal: Celebrate progress, encourage scaling, and anchor wealth-building in long-term thinking.

T his is the payoff. This is the part where your financial garden starts producing fruit and planting seeds for those who come after you. This is what all the earlier work was for.

Now your financial tree begins to bear fruit: steady growth, optional income, and the mindset shift from surviving to scaling. In this stage, we go beyond accumulation and step into intention and impact. You'll learn how to grow your systems, shape your legacy, and make your money move and grow with purpose.

Real wealth isn't just about what you build, it's about what you pass on that's more valuable than money -knowledge, habits, values, assets, freedom.

Chapter Thirty-Five

Scaling With Intention

Don't Just Grow, Grow On Purpose

You've done the groundwork, now it's time to grow with strategy, not speed. Let's be clear, we're not talking about chasing hot trends or throwing money at the latest get-rich-quick pitch. Scaling is not about speed, it's about structure. It's about making intentional decisions that multiply what's already working, without adding chaos. Most beginners think the next step after "investing" is "more investing." But real growth comes from:

- Deepening your conviction, not just expanding your exposure.

- Increasing contributions, not just adding complexity.

- Creating new systems to match your new goals.

This chapter marks the transition from managing money to multiplying it, from defense to offense.

Belief Flip:
Old Belief: "Growth means adding complexity."
New Belief: "Real growth simplifies your life, not complicates it."

The Garden Metaphor: Expanding Your Orchard
Your garden is thriving, but before you plant more trees, ask yourself:

- Is the soil (your system) ready to support more?

- Do you have the tools (automations, contributions, education) to tend to this next phase?

- Will this addition feed your goals, or distract from them?

The best investors don't just plant more, they plant better. Strategic growth means pruning what no longer fits and creating space for what's next.

How to Scale with Intention
Scaling is personal, but here are a few universal strategies to consider:

Scaling Strategy	Description
Increase Contributions	Easiest win: Boost your percentage in existing investment accounts.
Rebalance Portfolio	Adjust allocations to match your evolving risk tolerance, goals and age.
Broaden Exposure	Add sectors (tech, energy), vehicles (REITs, ETFs), asset classes (real estate, precious metals) or foreign regions (if it aligns).
Add Income Streams	Explore passive income or side investments to fund more contributions.
Refine Your Goals	Revisit your financial goals and timelines — are they growing with you?

Final Word: Multiply with Meaning
You're no longer just a saver or an investor, you're a strategic wealth builder. Moving forward, every decision you make has the power to feed not just your life...but your legacy. Continue to grow and scale with intention, not stress.

> **CIO Insight:** Scaling Requires a CIO Upgrade
> You're not running a side hustle; you're running your life like an enterprise. Growth demands a better operating system, not just in how you manage your accounts, but in your mindset. One of the best ways to do this is by investing in your education. The mindset, knowledge, and skills that got you to six figures won't get you to seven. Growth requires upgrading how you think before anything else.

Reflection Prompt
What does "scaling" mean to you...more money, more time, freedom, more impact? Where in your current plan can you grow intentionally?

Chapter Thirty-Six

Generational Wealth Starts With You

Build a Legacy You'd Be Proud to Receive

I f you're reading this, chances are you weren't handed a financial playbook growing up. You're planting the seeds for long-term wealth, not just for you, but for those who come next. This chapter isn't about leaving millions (though that wouldn't hurt), it's about leaving a map your loved ones can follow and build on.

Most people have the dream of leaving something behind. But as the saying goes, "A dream without a plan is just a hallucination." Wealth that lasts doesn't happen by accident; it happens on purpose through attention, intention, and consistent action. Whether it's financial, relational, or spiritual, real wealth is what lives on after you.

Belief Flip:
Old Belief: "Generational wealth is for the rich."
New Belief: "Generational wealth is within reach; it starts with intention, not income."

You don't need millions to pass on wealth. You need a strategy, a system, a set of values, and a vision. Pass the knowledge that wasn't passed to you, and the next generation can build a fortune.

4 Pillars of Generational Wealth

Pillar	Description	Example
Assets	Tangible wealth to pass on	Home equity, life insurance, investments, business ownership
Access	Tools, connections, or privileges	College fund, mentorship, professionasl, networks
Education	Financial literacy and mindset	Teaching kids about saving, investing, and taxes
Identity	Family values, vision, and culture	"In our family, we build. We don't waste."

Start small, but think big. Even a simple Roth IRA can change your child's trajectory, if it comes with the story of why it exists.

Final Word: Pass the Torch, Not Just the Tools

This is legacy, not luxury. This is freedom, not flex. In addition to focusing on what you leave behind, focus on what you build in the people who'll carry your legacy. The fruit trees that matter most, are the ones that continue to produce after you're gone.

CIO Insight: You're Not Just a Provider, You're a Path Builder. A major part of generational wealth is about modeling – having conversations, sharing habits, beliefs, and stories that your kids or loved ones can "inherit" and carry forward. Be the person they quote when they make their first investment. Be the one built the systems they follow. You don't need to be perfect – just intentional. Let the next generation perfect what you started.

Reflection Prompt

What do you wish someone had taught you about money growing up? What can you do today to ensure your kids (or nieces/ nephews/ godchildren) learn that lesson sooner?

Chapter Thirty-Seven

Creating Your Wealth Cycle

The System That Sets You Free

You've been doing the work! You've planted the seeds, built your system, weathered the storms, and stayed consistent. And now... you're starting to see the fruit. Maybe not all at once, but the ground has shifted beneath you. Here's the "secret sauce" part of the journey we've taken together. While you thought you were just learning to invest...

You were building a Wealth Cycle.

What Is a Wealth Cycle?

In Stage 3, we introduced you to a hard truth most people don't see coming: **Your income isn't the problem; it's your flow that requires attention first.** That's when we first revealed the "Working Poor Cycle," a painful, repeating pattern where your money disappears before it ever has a chance to build wealth. You work hard, pay taxes, pay bills, swipe cards, and then wait for the next paycheck. During that wait, you're hoping there aren't more days in the month than dollars in your account. That's not a financial plan, that's survival on a hamster wheel.

When you are trapped in the Working Poor Cycle:

- You trade your time for money (job).

- Taxes take the first 25–35%.

- Bills and debts take the rest.

- You try to survive until next payday.

- Any emergency wipes out progress.

- You repeat.

No wiggle room. No flexibility. No room to invest. It's a constant financial redlining. None of this is by accident... It's the trap... It's by design... Do not forget: "Every system is perfectly designed to get the results it gets." - W. Edwards Deming

J.O.B. – This Isn't a Coincidence.

As a quick aside, have you ever stopped and thought about what J.O.B. really stands for? It stands for what the system is designed to do: keep you Just Over Broke.

- Just over broke... so you're too tired to revolt, but just comfortable enough to comply.

- Just over broke... so you're always needing the job more than it needs you.

- Just over broke... because the system runs best when labor is cheap and dreams are small.

- Just over broke... so your boss pays you just enough to keep you showing up, but never enough to break free.

- Just over broke... because your struggle keeps shareholder profits fat and expenses low.

- Just over broke... because when you're stuck in the Working Poor Cycle, escape feels impossible.

The system was designed to keep you stuck.
The Wealth Cycle is designed to set you free.

We showed you how to Break the Working Poor Cycle, we showed you the off-ramps:

- **Pay Yourself First.**

- **Redirect the Flow.**

- **Automate the Habit.**

- **Reclaim your future.**

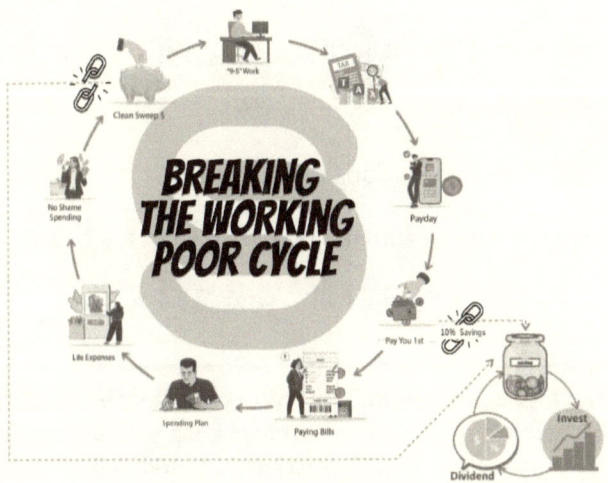

What you may not have realized is that every single chapter in every Stage has quietly been building something bigger. Every worksheet, every tool, every shift in your system and mindset has been guiding you toward a larger structure, your Wealth Cycle, designed to do one thing:

SET YOU FREE!

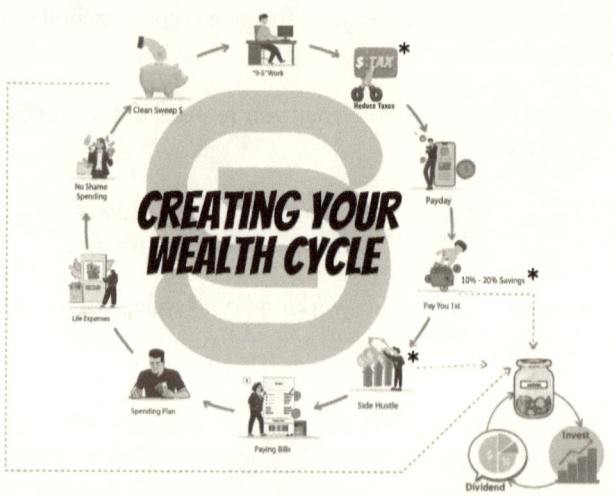

This is the moment where the dots connect, like Daniel-San realizing "wax-on" and "wax-off" wasn't just a chore, it was training.

- You weren't just paying yourself first.

- You weren't just budgeting.

- You weren't just cutting expenses.

- You weren't just picking investments.

- You weren't just automating savings and a few bills.

- You were building a system... **your Wealth Cycle.**

Breaking the Cycle in Action: The Habits Behind the Wealth Cycle
The Wealth Cycle begins when you start managing your money, and your life, differently. Each step of the cycle replaces an old survival behavior with a new wealth behavior. Here's how it works in practice:

- **Reduce Taxes.** Keeping more of what you earn is one of the most overlooked parts of building wealth. Taxes are one of the biggest expenses you'll face over your lifetime, so tax efficiency has to be built into your Wealth Cycle. Use pre-tax vehicles like retirement accounts, HSAs, or FSAs to lower your taxable income. Every dollar you keep from "Uncle Sam" is another employee you can deploy toward your financial freedom.

- **Pay Yourself First**. You've seen this before; it's your first major breakthrough. It shifts your focus from survival spending to self-prioritization. Every dollar gets a job before it has a chance to disappear. You become the boss, not your bills.

- **Add A Side Hustle.** A side hustle isn't about grinding 24/7, it's about creating breathing room. When you earn more, you give your Wealth Cycle more fuel to work with. That extra income can accelerate debt payoff, boost your investments, or fund your next goal. Start with what you know, what you enjoy, or what solves a problem for others. Whether it's freelancing, selling products, or offering a service, remember: every dollar earned outside your main job is a freedom dollar as it speeds up your path to wealth.

- **A Spending Plan** (Spending with Intention). Budgets can feel restrictive, but a spending plan puts you back in control. A spending plan is different; it's a mindset shift from "What can I cut?" to "Where do I want it to go?" Now you're asking a better question: "What deserves my dollars?" When you spend according to your values instead of your moods, money becomes a tool, not a temptation.

- **No Shame Spending.** For most, this is a mini freedom moment. Once you've paid yourself first and covered your essentials, the rest is No Shame Spending. You've done the work and now you get to enjoy your money without guilt. True discipline isn't about deprivation; it's about direction.

- **Eliminate Unconscious Spending.** Unconscious spending is where most people leak their future wealth. Unused subscriptions, convenience splurges, emotional swipes — all those "small" things quietly erode your freedom. Removing this reflexive habit closes one of the biggest drains in your Wealth Cycle. As CIO, your job is to stay alert so you don't accidentally lose employees (dollars) that should still be on your payroll.

- **The Clean Sweep.** As previously mentioned, this is your monthly reset. The final move that keeps you disciplined. At the end of each month, right before you receive your next paycheck, sweep whatever's left in your checking account into savings or investments. You remove idle money before it tempts you back into old habits. It's how you close the loop and prove to yourself that the Wealth Cycle is real and active.

Building wealth isn't about one big move; it's about creating a system and rhythm that repeats itself. Every paycheck, every decision, every habit inside this cycle compounds over time. When you protect your incomes from taxes, pay yourself first, spend with intention, eliminate waste, and sweep your leftovers toward growth, you're no longer reacting, you're leading. This is how the shift happens. Money starts serving a very different role in your life and you uncover the path to wealth and freedom. It's how the wealthy escape the paycheck-to-paycheck life. It's how they turn money into more money. The Wealth Cycle isn't theory; it's the daily proof that you've taken control, broken the old cycle, and started living on purpose.

Signs of a Maximized Wealth Cycle
Below are the telltale signs that your financial system is moving from hustle... to harvest. This list might feel advanced, and that's okay; you're still a beginner. The point isn't to master every part today, but to see what's possible when your system matures.

- **You earn income**

- **Minimize taxes using:**
  Pre-tax investments.☐
  Pre-tax health savings.☐
  Accurate paycheck withholdings.☐
  Side-hustle expenses and deductions.☐
  Maximizing tax breaks.☐
  Reducing capital gains tax.

- **Automatically pay yourself first 10-20%**

- **Invest consistently.**

- **Reinvest what your investments earn and letting the cycle repeat.**

- **Generate additional income (business/side-hustle).**

- **Reduced expenses and liabilities.**

- **Following a spending plan.**

- **Spending without shame.**

- **Redirecting unspent funds into savings or investments.**

Over time, the system runs with or without you, and that's how you finally escape the hamster wheel. **It's all Interconnected.**

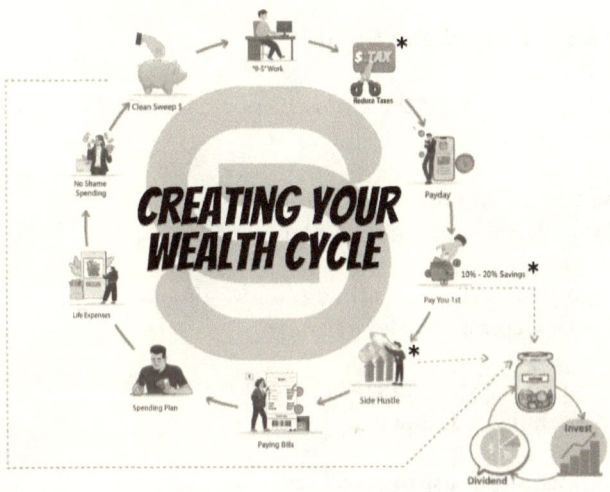

Both Good and Bad: Everything is connected. Bad spending habits mean fewer dollars to invest... No investments keep you on the hamster wheel longer... Living above your means leads to more debt... More debt leads to more stress... Stress impacts your happiness... This convinces you that buying "something nice" will make you feel better, which in turns leads to more spending, starting the vicious cycle all over again. That's why the CIO mindset matters, because as CIO, your job is to see the full picture and make sure all the pieces are working together. From there, you begin optimizing every part of your Wealth Cycle.

CIO Insight:
A maximized Wealth Cycle isn't about effort; it's about designing a system that runs on autopilot. Hustle can start the engine, but structure keeps it running. The goal isn't working harder; but to create a system so dialed in that your money grows and compounds without constant supervision. That's CIO-level leadership. When your cycle is optimized, wealth isn't earned dollar-by-dollar; it's built layer by layer. Just like a well-planted garden draws nutrients from the soil, your system keeps growing and flourishing even when you're not tending to it.

Why the Wealth Cycle Matters
Without it, being poor becomes a loop you can't escape, no matter how hard you work. You can make six figures and still feel broke. When you have a wealth cycle, every dollar has a job, every system supports the next, and your financial life compounds even while you sleep.

Your Wealth Cycle is your business plan, and as CIO, you must manage every part.

How This Book Helped You Build It
Here's how it all fits together: Every stage you've completed was part of a bigger plan, preparing you to build the mindset, systems, and habits that make your Wealth Cycle run.

Stage 1 gave you the mindset and identity shift
(CIO thinking, Belief Flips, internal alignment)

Stage 2 taught you the power of time and investing basics
(Seeds + growth = compound leverage)

Stage 3 helped with systems of automation/consistency
(Water the garden. Keep it flowing.)

Stage 4 equipped you for storms and setbacks
(Don't panic. Stay planted. Think long-term.)

Stage 5 was about scaling, passing it on, and leading
(Growth → Fruit → Legacy)

And with this final section, you realize that you weren't just learning to invest, **you were learning how to build your Wealth Cycle.**

The 6 Gears of the Wealth Cycle
Every Wealth Cycle runs on a set of critical components. If even one slips, the whole system can grind to a halt, but when they work in harmony, your goal of wealth becomes undeniable.

Let's break them down:

Gear	What It Does	Your Leverage Point
Income	The money you earn	Grow your skills, start a side hustle, ask for a raise
Spending	Where your money goes	Align spending to values; cut leaks, not joy
Saving	Your financial buffer	Automate savings before spending; build stability
Investing	Your money working for you	Pay yourself first and invest early/often
Debt Management	What you owe and why	Eliminate toxic debt, leverage good debt
Tax Optimization	What you keep after Uncle Sam	Use legal strategies to reduce taxes and grow wealth faster

Most people live reactively; wealth-building CIOs engineer this cycle on purpose.

The Fuel That Keeps the Cycle Going
Even the best-designed cycle won't run without fuel; and in your financial life, that fuel is emotional energy. Change doesn't happen just because you read a good book. It happens when you get **sick and tired of being sick and tired.** It happens when you look at your current financial reality and say, **"This is no longer acceptable."**

That was the moment my life changed. It wasn't because I learned something new about finances, budgets or investing. Most people believe all they need is a little more information and that will make the difference. Here's the reality: **if all it took was information, we'd all be happy, healthy, and wealthy.** My lack of success wasn't about knowing what to "DO." It was about learning how to "BE" the person who could consistently do what was needed. For me, the lasting shift occurred when I got fed up. Fed up with being broke. Fed up with living the way I was living. Fed up with watching the system eat up my time and give me crumbs in return.

That fire. That pain. That hunger. That "I'm so over this" moment – that decision to never go back... that's what gave me the drive to build my Wealth Cycle, especially when I didn't feel like it. When motivation fades... When the road forward feels too hard to continue. You need something more powerful; that something is "YOUR WHY!"

Your "WHY" can't be squishy or vague; it must be clear and highly desirable. Ideally, your "why" should feel as important to you as your next breath of air.

When your "why" is that powerful, obstacles become stepping stones instead of roadblocks, and moments of doubt become opportunities to reassure yourself of your commitment to your goal. Your "why" is not just your reason; it is your fuel, your compass, and your fire. Whether you're driven to escape pain or pursue pleasure, what is important is that you keep stoking that fire.

> Don't lose sight of your reason. Write it down. Keep it close. Revisit it often. The Wealth Cycle is the machine, but your "why"? That supplies the fuel that keeps the fire burning.

Journal Prompts
Now that you understand the system, take a moment to reconnect with your motivation.

- What's your "Why"?

- What are you building toward that's bigger than your current struggle?

- Why is this so important to you?   What are you willing to do?

- What commitments are you ready to make and keep?

- What kind of freedom do you want to feel?

Reflection Questions
- What does my current wealth cycle look like?

- Where are the leaks?

- Which gears (income, spending, saving, investing, debt, taxes) needs the most attention right now?

- What's one small change I can make to start reinforcing my system this week?

- What does breaking the working poor cycle mean for me and my family?

- Am I operating like the CIO or like an employee of the system?

Final Thought
Wealth isn't built in isolation; it's built-in cycles. You've planted the seeds; now it's time to let your system grow.

Chapter Thirty-Eight

Putting It Into Motion

Time to Put Your Money to Work and Start the Process!

You made it! You got this guide... You showed up... You pushed past the doubt... You read every chapter, wrestled with old beliefs, and reprogrammed your money mindset. You're not the same person who started this guide. So now it's time:

Time to plant. Time to move. Time to invest like your future depends on it, because it does.

> Nothing changes until you do... and it requires you to A.C.T. because Action Changes Things.

So, here's the final push, a simple, clear plan to go from "learning" to "launching."

Your 7-Step Quick Start Plan

1. Activate A.C.T. (Action Changes Things)□
Les Brown said it best: "It's the start that stops most people." Don't wait to feel 100% ready. Start now. Time is your superpower, and every dollar you delay is a dollar that never compounds. Every day you delay, the less time your dollars have to compound.

2. Choose One Clear Goal
What are you building toward? Retirement? A down payment? Financial freedom? Clarity fuels consistency. Write it down and aim your plan at that target.

3. Build a Mini Emergency Fund
You can't invest with confidence if you're constantly bracing for the next bill. Get $1,000 in a savings buffer, then build to 3–6 months over time. This is your garden's protective fence.

4. Open Your First Investment Account
Pick a brokerage account... Don't overthink it! Just get in the game.

5. Automate Your Contributions
This is your wealth engine. Set up automatic transfers at least monthly. Consistency beats intensity... $50/WK beats $500 you never invest.

6. Pick Your First Investment
Start with a low-cost index fund or ETF. Don't chase hype. Don't try to time the market. Begin with the boring stuff because it's how real wealth is built. (Need help? Use an online robo-advisor.)

7. Celebrate...Then Keep Going.□
Celebrate your little wins along the way, you're rewriting your family's financial story. This is the moment you stop reacting to money, step into your power, and start directing it with purpose.

Reflection Prompt
What's your first next step? Open an account? Set up automation? Choose your first investment? Write it down, set a deadline, and honor it.

CIO Reflection: What's one part of your money system – how money flows in, out, and gets invested – that you'll improve this quarter? What will it require of you, and how committed are you to making it happen?

Final Word: You're Not a Beginner Anymore
You're now better prepared than most investors. You've got the tools, the truth, and a plan that works. You know what matters and what doesn't. So don't just let this book sit on a shelf (digital or physical). Now's the time to build. Move. Invest. Multiply. Because your future self is already proud of the moves you're about to make.

Lead your finances with purpose, protect what you've planted, and keep stacking – your future self is counting on you.

Let's get it started.

Chapter Thirty-Nine

Tools

Activity #1: Scaling Strategy Planner

S caling isn't about doing more; it's about building smarter. Use this planner to take inventory of where you are, where you're growing, and what needs upgrading in your system.

STEP 1: Inventory Your Current Setup
Quick check-in to see how solid your foundation is before scaling.

Area	My Current Setup (Describe Briefly)	Confidence Level (√ Low, √ Med, √ High)
Monthly Investment Contributions		□ Low □ Med □ High
Investment Accounts Open		□ Low □ Med □ High
Portfolio Allocation		□ Low □ Med □ High
Asset Exposure (Sectors, Assets)		□ Low □ Med □ High
Automation & Transfers		□ Low □ Med □ High
Review & Rebalancing Schedule		□ Low □ Med □ High
Financial Education Routine		□ Low □ Med □ High

STEP 2: Identify Your Scaling Opportunities
Choose where you want to grow, and how.

Scaling Strategy	Description	Will I Do This?	Target Action Date	Notes or Next Step
Increase Contributions	Increase monthly contributions	☐ Yes ☐ No		
Rebalance Portfolio	Adjust allocation to match new goals or age	☐ Yes ☐ No		
Expand Asset Exposure	Add REITs, international, or new sectors	☐ Yes ☐ No		
Add Income Streams	Build passive income to increase investable cash	☐ Yes ☐ No		
Level Up Your Education	Read, take a course, or attend a workshop	☐ Yes ☐ No		
Revisit Financial Goals	Update or clarify short- and long-term goals	☐ Yes ☐ No		
Upgrade Financial Tools	Try new budgeting apps, dashboards, or software	☐ Yes ☐ No		

STEP 3: Define Your Scaling Vision
Write a short paragraph that captures your next-level money move. This is your why for scaling.

I want to scale my financial system so that I can_____, without feeling_____. My next financial level looks like ___and I'm committed to ___starting today.

***

Activity #2: Wealth Plan Launch Pad
Your 1-Page Quick Start Checklist: Pin it. Print it. Put it to work

Step 1: Commit to A.C.T. (Action Changes Things)☐
Pick a date. Make the move. Start with what you know.

My Start Date:

Step 2: Set One Clear Goal
What are you investing for?

- Retirement

- Homeownership

- Time Freedom

- Kids' Education

- Other:

Step 3: Build a Mini Emergency Fund
Start with $1,000. Then build to 3–6 months. My Starting Fund Target: $

Step 4: Open Your First Account
Choose one to begin:

- Roth IRA

- Traditional IRA

- 401(k)

- Brokerage Account

- Robo-Advisor Platform

- Other:

Step 5: Automate Your Contributions
Pick your rhythm:

- Weekly

- Biweekly

- Monthly

- Other:

Automatic Amount: $

Step 6: Choose Your First Investment(s)
- Index Fund (e.g., S&P 500)

- Total Market ETF

- Target-Date Fund

- Dividend ETF

- Robo-Advisor Portfolio

- Other:

Step 7: Schedule a Review
Put a date on the calendar for your first portfolio check-in. My Review Date:

Step 8: Keep Learning
- Subscribe to financial YouTube channels (like Stackers U)

- Read one book this quarter

- Join a community or mastermind

- Teach someone what you learned My Next Move:

Final Reminder: Done is better than perfect!
Start small. Stay consistent. Stack steady. Scale forever. This is your launch!

NEXT MOVES

YOU'RE NOT A BEGINNER ANYMORE

STACKERS UNIVERSITY

Stackers University

Chapter Forty

You're Different Now!

Theme: Lead the Legacy. Play the Long Game. Goal: Celebrate the transformation, reinforce life-long habits, and inspire next steps.

P ause for a second and take this in: You made it. Not just to the end of a book, but to the beginning of a brand-new identity. You've planted seeds, weathered storms, tended to your money, built systems that work, and learned to protect your mindset. You've gone from a passive consumer of financial advice to the CIO of your financial life, someone who leads their money.

That's not small... That's monumental.

Because now, you're the Chief Investment Officer of your life, and that means you've shifted from reacting to money, to leading it. Your identity has changed. Too many people think wealth-building starts with a brokerage account, but after this journey, you now know it starts with something deeper: **a commitment to your future self and the life you want to build.**

This mindset shift journey we've taken you on is one of the biggest game changers when it comes to building wealth. As we shared earlier, the path to wealth: "It's not easy, but it's simple." While the tasks of paying yourself first, spending less than you make, and investing may be straightforward to understand, putting it into practice can be very difficult if you haven't done the internal work. That's the game of wealth in a nutshell: It all starts in your head.

As the philosopher Friedrich Nietzsche said, "He who has a why to live can bear almost any how." The same is true for building wealth. If your reason, your why, is strong enough, you'll find the discipline to follow through on the how. When the grind gets tough or the 'YOLO' (You Only Live Once) mindset tries to hijack your efforts, return to your purpose. That "WHY" is your anchor. It's what gives you the resilience to push through discomfort, delay gratification, and to keep going, especially when quitting feels easier.

Now that you've upgraded from treating money like an afterthought to leading it like a business owner, your mindset has to focus on building your wealth cycle. Ensuring your money flows through a purpose-built system, rather than randomness or reaction.

As you've learned, the key to investing success is about how you think, what you believe, and how you behave when money is on the line. That is what changes everything, for you, and for the next generation.

Stay the Course
You've built the foundation. Now it's time to protect and refine it.

- **Annual Reviews:** Set a calendar date to review your goals, portfolio, and contributions. Make it a ritual, not a reaction.

- **Rebalancing:** Markets shift and allocations change over time.

- Realign your portfolio as your strategy or life changes.

- **Check-ins:** Every 3–6 months, ask: Is my money still working toward my priorities? Am I still playing offense, or drifting into defense?

- **Habit Tracking:** Small behaviors = big results. Automate what you can. Track what you can't.

- **System Upgrades:** As your income grows or life changes, your financial system should evolve too. Don't stay stuck in a version of life you've outgrown.

Do these things consistently, and your system won't just sustain you, it'll free you.

Wealth isn't about doing more — it's about repeating what works.

Final Word: From Seed to Strategy
You've stepped into your leadership role as the CIO of You, Inc. When we began this journey, the idea of thinking and acting like a Chief Investment Officer might've felt foreign. But look at you now: analyzing assets, managing cash flow, assessing risk, and building a system where every dollar is an employee working toward your freedom. You're not just saving or spending anymore; you're directing capital with intention. That's what a CIO does.

Don't forget: this journey has always been about planting seeds. As a gardener, you've learned to respect the process: plant what matters, water it consistently, and stay patient through every season. You now understand that wealth doesn't happen overnight; it grows underground before it blossoms in real life. The roots you've built: mentally, emotionally, and strategically, will support your growth for decades to come. This guide taught you how to:

- Structure your money like a business.

- Build systems that automate your wealth.

- Choose investments that match your timeline and temperament.

- Face risk without fear.

- Stay grounded during emotional storms.

- And define financial freedom on your own terms.

So what's next?

Keep planting. Keep leading. Keep growing.

Because now you're not just the CIO of your finances.

You're the head gardener of your future. You're the author of your legacy.

And every dollar you direct, every decision you make, every seed you plant,

It's not just changing your life... it's changing your family tree.

From here, the mission is simple (but not always easy)!

You're the CIO now – Make your legacy undeniable.

Chapter Forty-One

Tools

Activity #1: Final Reflection – Look How Far You've Come

You didn't just read a book... You rewired your thinking... You planted seeds... You showed up for your future self. Now it's time to look in the mirror and honor the shift. Use this space to document the transformation: in mindset, confidence, and strategy. This is your snapshot in time. One day, you'll look back and realize... this was the moment everything started to change.

Today's Date:

What I Now Know About Money That I Didn't Before:
Example: "Time is my most powerful asset." "I can design a system, not rely on willpower."

My #1 Money Habit I'm Most Proud Of:
Example: "I started automating my investing." "I finally paid myself first."

The Mindset Shift That Changed Everything:
Example: "I'm the CIO of my life." "Investing is about identity, not just income."

The Wealth I Want to Build Isn't Just for Me. It's For:
Example: "My kids." "My peace of mind." "Generations I'll never meet."

My Commitment Moving Forward:

What promise are you making to your future self, starting now?
"I will... I will no longer... I will always"

Sign it. Date it. Own it.

Signature:_____ Date:_____

Activity #2: My Money Manifesto
Because Wealth Without Clarity is Just Noise.

This is your stake in the ground. A declaration of the kind of investor and person you've chosen to become. Not just for today, but for the life you're building.

My Core Money Beliefs
Write 3–5 beliefs that guide how you think about money and investing. Examples: "Money is a tool, not a trophy." "Investing is an act of leadership." "Time is more valuable than income."

1.

2.

3.

4.

5.

My Wealth Priorities
What really matters to you? What are you building toward? Examples: Freedom, security, options, legacy, peace of mind, impact, time.

1.

2.

3.

The Values That Guide Me
How do you want to show up with your money? In the way you spend, invest, and plan? Examples: Discipline, generosity, wisdom, stewardship, intentionality, and patience.

1.

2.

3.

My Wealth-Building Code

Write your own short credo or code — like a personal mission statement for your financial life. Example: "I use money to build freedom, not flex. I invest with intention, not impulse. I grow wealth for impact, not ego. I protect my peace and play the long game."

Signature & Commitment

I commit to leading my financial life with clarity, courage, and consistency. This manifesto is a living document, and I reserve the right to grow, refine, and evolve. But my commitment to wealth with purpose will never change.

Signature:_____ Date:_____

APPENDICES

Stackers University

Chapter Forty-Two

Appendix A: Glossary of Terms

Quick Reference for Financial Terms and Investing Lingo.

Core Investment Terms

- **Asset**: Anything you own that has value or puts money in your pocket.

- **Liability**: A debt or obligation that takes money out of your pocket.

- **Net Worth**: Your total assets minus your total liabilities – a snapshot of your financial health.

- **Stock**: A share of ownership in a company.

- **Bond**: A loan you make to a company or government that pays interest.

- **ETF (Exchange-Traded Fund)**: A collection of investments that trades like a stock.

- **Mutual Fund**: A pooled investment that buys a variety of assets.

- **REIT (Real Estate Investment Trust)**: A company that owns and manages income-producing real estate that pays dividends to investors.

Market Mechanics & Orders

- **Ask Price:** The lowest price a seller is willing to accept.

- **Bid Price:** The highest price a buyer is willing to pay.

- **Market Order:** Buy/sell immediately at the best price.

- **Limit Order:** Buy/sell only at your specified price or better.

- **Settlement Period**: The time it takes for a trade to finalize (usually T+2).

- **Liquidity**: How easily an investment can be converted to cash.

- **Commission**: A fee charged by a broker per trade.

- **Expense Ratio**: Annual fee charged by a fund, shown as a percentage of assets.

Investment Strategies & Practices

- **Diversification**: Spreading your money across assets to reduce risk.

- **Asset Allocation**: Dividing your portfolio between different asset classes (e.g., stocks, bonds, cash).

- **Dollar-Cost Averaging:** Investing the same amount regularly, regardless of market conditions.

- **Rebalancing**: Adjusting your portfolio to stay aligned with your original plan.

- **Passive Investing:** A buy-and-hold strategy using index funds or ETFs.

- **Active Investing:** Trying to beat the market through timing or picking specific assets.

- **Robo-Advisor**: A digital platform that uses algorithms to invest for you.

Retirement & Savings Accounts

- **IRA (Individual Retirement Account)**: A tax-advantaged way to save for retirement.

- **Roth IRA:** Funded with after-tax dollars; withdrawals are tax-free.

- **Traditional IRA:** Funded with pre-tax dollars; taxed upon withdrawal.

- **401(k):** Employer-sponsored retirement plan with tax-deferred growth.

- **CD (Certificate of Deposit):** A savings product that locks your money in for a fixed term at a fixed interest rate.

- **Money Market Account:** A savings account with higher yields and limited check-writing ability.

Income, Returns & Taxes

- **Dividend:** A portion of a company's profits paid to shareholders.

- **Capital Gains**: Profit from selling an asset at a higher price than the purchase.

- **Yield:** The income return on an investment, shown as a percentage.

- **Tax-Loss Harvesting:** Selling losing investments to offset capital gains and reduce taxes.

- **Qualified Dividend:** A dividend taxed at the lower capital gains rate.

- **Ordinary Income**: Earnings taxed at your regular income rate.

Risk & Market Behavior

- **Risk Tolerance**: How much risk you can emotionally and financially handle.

- **Market Volatility**: The speed and amount of price changes in the market.

- **Bear Market**: When prices fall by 20% or more.

- **Bull Market**: When prices rise with optimism and momentum.

- **Drawdown:** A peak-to-trough decline in investment value before recovery.

Smart Money Moves (Stackers Framework & Mindset)

- **Financial Blueprint:** Your personalized investing game plan based on values, goals, and systems.

- **Wealth Cycle:** A self-sustaining flow of money from income to investing and back.

- **CIO (Chief Investment Officer):** The mindset of taking full ownership of your financial decisions and strategy.

- **Automated Wealth System**: A set of rules and tools to put your money on autopilot.

- **Investing Identity**: The beliefs, behaviors, and confidence you develop as a committed investor.

- **Behavioral Triggers:** Emotional responses (fear, greed, FOMO) that lead to impulsive financial decisions.

- **Stacking with Intention:** Choosing to grow wealth in alignment with your values and capacity — not just chasing returns.

- **Mental Rebalancing:** Adjusting not just your portfolio, but your mindset, when circumstances change

- **Legacy Leadership:** Building wealth with the purpose of passing on values, assets, and vision — not just money.

Chapter Forty-Three

Appendix B: Summary of Core ETFs

Category	ETF	Provider	Expense Ratio	10-Yr Avg Return
S&P 500	VOO	Vanguard	0.03%	12.46%
	IVV	iShares	0.03%	Similar to VOO
	SPY	State Street	0.09%	Similar to VOO
	SCHX	Schwab	0.03%	Similar to VOO
	FXAIX	Fidelity	0.02%	Similar to VOO
US Total Market	VTI	Vanguard	0.03%	11.74%
	ITOT	iShares	0.03%	Similar to VTI
	SPTM	State Street	0.03%	Similar to VTI
	SCHB	Schwab	0.03%	Similar to VTI
	FZROX	Fidelity	0.00%	Similar to VTI
Dividend	SCHD	Schwab	0.06%	11.43%
	VYM	Vanguard	0.06%	N/A
	DGRO	iShares	0.08%	N/A
	SDY	State Street	0.35%	N/A
	FDVV	Fidelity	0.29%	N/A

Category	ETF	Provider	Expense Ratio	10-Yr Avg Return
Dividend	SCHD	Schwab	0.06%	11.43%
	VYM	Vanguard	0.06%	N/A
	DGRO	iShares	0.08%	N/A
	SDY	State Street	0.35%	N/A
	FDVV	Fidelity	0.29%	N/A
Growth	VGT	Vanguard	0.09%	18.93%
	QQQ	Invesco	0.20%	16.99%
	VUG	Vanguard	0.04%	N/A
	IVW	iShares	0.18%	N/A
	SPYG	State Street	0.04%	N/A
	SCHG	Schwab	0.04%	N/A
	FSPGX	Fidelity	0.04%	N/A

Category	ETF	Provider	Expense Ratio	10-Yr Avg Return
Value	VTV	Vanguard	0.04%	N/A
	IVE	iShares	0.18%	N/A
	SPYV	State Street	0.04%	N/A
	SCHV	Schwab	0.04%	N/A
	FSPVX	Fidelity	0.04%	N/A
Mid-Cap	VO	Vanguard	0.04%	N/A
	IJH	iShares	0.06%	N/A
	MDY	State Street	0.23%	N/A
	SCHM	Schwab	0.04%	N/A
Small-Cap	VB	Vanguard	0.06%	N/A
	IJR	iShares	0.06%	N/A
	SPSM	State Street	0.05%	N/A
	SCHA	Schwab	0.04%	N/A

Category	ETF	Provider	Expense Ratio	10-Yr Avg Return
International (Ex-US)	VXUS	Vanguard	0.07%	5.24%
	IXUS	iShares	0.07%	Similar to VXUS
	CWI	State Street	0.30%	N/A
	SCHF	Schwab	0.06%	N/A
Global Stocks	VT	Vanguard	0.07%	8.91%
	URTH	iShares	0.24%	N/A
	SPGM	State Street	0.09%	N/A
Bonds (Core US)	BND	Vanguard	0.03%	1.33%
	AGG	iShares	0.03%	1.28%
	SCHZ	Schwab	0.04%	Similar to BND
	FBND	Fidelity	0.25%	Active management
	FXNAX	Fidelity	0.03%	Similar to BND

ETF & Index Fund Cheat Sheet

Fund Type	What It Tracks	Why It Matters	Common Examples	When to Use
Total Market Fund	Entire U.S. stock market (large, mid, and small-cap companies)	Broad exposure, great for beginners, captures overall growth of U.S. economy	VTI (Vanguard), ITOT (iShares), FZROX (Fidelity)	When you want to keep it simple and diversified in one fund
S&P 500 Index Fund	Top 500 U.S. companies by market cap	Focused on large, stable companies, historical backbone of investing	SPY (ETF), VOO (Vanguard), FXAIX (Fidelity index fund)	When you want big-name exposure with lower volatility
Dividend ETF	Stocks that regularly pay dividends	Generates passive income with capital growth possible	VYM (Vanguard), SCHD (Schwab), DVY (iShares)	For income in retirement or to reinvest dividends
Bond ETF	U.S. government or corporate bonds	Adds stability, reduces risk, buffers stock market dips	BND (Total Bond), AGG (iShares Core), TLT (Long-term Treasury)	To balance risk or create a safer income stream
International ETF	Developed or emerging markets outside the U.S.	Adds global diversification, potential growth in rising economies	VXUS (Vanguard Total Intl), VEU (All-World ex-US), IEMG (Emerging Markets)	When you want exposure to global markets
Thematic/Sector ETF	Specific industries (tech, energy, real estate, etc.)	Targeted bets on sectors you believe in or want to overweight	XLK (Tech), XLE (Energy), VNQ (Real Estate)	When you want to express a strong view or tilt your portfolio
Target Date Fund	Adjusts allocation based on retirement year	"Set it and forget it" option. Auto-adjusts from growth to safety	VTTSX (Vanguard 2060), FDEWX (Fidelity 2055)	When you want one fund that evolves with you

---

Chapter Forty-Four

Appendix C: Nota Bene

Principles to Carry Forward

This appendix isn't a checklist or a set of new steps. It's a reminder of what matters most, the truths worth writing on your mirror or taping to your desk. *Nota bene* is Latin for "note well." In old manuscripts, scholars scribbled it in the margins to flag the ideas too important to forget. Consider this appendix your margin notes for wealth-building. The essentials to revisit when life or the markets get noisy.

These principles are the seeds and roots of your financial garden: simple, sturdy truths that keep growing when watered with consistency. As CIO, you don't need to memorize every detail of this book, but you do need to anchor to the ideas that shape identity and direct behavior. That's what this section gives you: portable truths short enough to remember, strong enough to guide you, and steady enough to return to when emotions or circumstances get messy.

Carry these *nota bene* with you. Let them be your compass: keeping you aligned, focused, resilient, and growing long after you've closed the last page.

Stage 1 – Preparing the Soil

- **"It's never about how much you make; it's about how much you spend."** As CIO, your revenue doesn't matter if your expenses devour it; the soil of wealth is stewardship, not income.

- **"When your outflow exceeds your income, your upkeep becomes your downfall." – Jim Rohn.** Just as a garden dies when more is pulled than replenished, a household collapses when spending outruns inflow.

- **"It's not about being an investor, it's about being the type of person that can invest."** Identity drives behavior; as CIO, who you are determines what grows in your financial garden.

- **"Every system is perfectly designed to get the results it gets."** If your garden isn't producing fruit, don't blame the seeds; redesign the system. – **W. Edwards Deming:**

- **"It's the start that stops most people." "You don't have to know everything in order to start. But you do have to start."** – **Les Brown** Growth never begins until the first seed is planted; don't wait for perfect conditions.

Stage 2 – Planting the Seeds

- **"Time is your superpower, and every dollar you delay is a dollar that never compounds."** The gardener who plants early reaps more seasons; as CIO, your edge is starting now, not later.

- **"An investment in knowledge pays the best interest."** – **Benjamin Franklin.** The first seeds in your financial garden are understanding and wisdom. Seeds of knowledge compound just like money; as CIO, the more you learn, the greater your harvest.

- **"Consistency beats intensity...$50/week beats $500 you never invest."** Watering a little every day builds roots; wealth grows from steady deposits, not occasional splashes.

Stage 3 – Designing the Garden

- **"The wealthy don't wait to save what's left. They save first, spend second."** Seeds go in the ground before they go to the table; investing comes before consumption.

- **"Wealth isn't about how much you make; it's about how much you keep."** Seeds wasted don't multiply; savings preserved can grow. A garden cannot survive if more is taken than given; neither can your wealth.

- **"Paying yourself first isn't just a strategy, it's a statement."** Gardeners eat after planting; as CIO, prioritizing yourself signals that wealth-building is non-negotiable.

- **"It's not easy, but it's simple.** A garden grows when you plant, water, and wait — not because you master complexity."

Stage 4 – Weathering the Seasons

- **"Wealth isn't built in isolation, it's built in cycles."** Winter and spring always return; markets and money follow seasons too. As CIO, your task is to endure, not to escape.

- **"If I don't manage my emotions, my emotions will manage my money."** Panic pulls up healthy plants; fear uproots good investments. Discipline keeps you steady when storms hit.

- **"Discipline beats emotion every time."** Gardeners don't panic in a storm; they protect their roots. investors don't panic in a dip; they trust their plan.

Stage 5 – The Fruit-Bearing Tree

- **"You're building a Wealth Cycle...a system."** A fruit tree grows because the system of soil, sun, and water repeats; as a CIO, wealth grows because you've built repeatable systems.

- **"Your 'why' is the fuel; the Wealth Cycle is the machine."** Seeds sprout when the gardener shows up; systems endure when CIOs stay committed.

- **"J.O.B. = Just Over Broke."** A gardener living off someone else's harvest will never be free; as CIO, you grow your own.

- **"The Wealth Cycle is designed to set you free."** True systems liberate; the more your cycle repeats, the less you depend on external control.

- **"Action Changes Things (A.C.T.)."** Nothing grows until something is planted; as CIO, every choice to act reshapes the harvest.

What you believe and think will always outwork what you know. Systems follow mindset. Habits follow belief. Every financial breakthrough begins with a thought strong enough to survive resistance. Let these truths rebuild the way you think, because once your mind is free, the rest of your wealth will follow.

The market will change. Your income, your goals, your seasons will change. But truth doesn't. When fear creeps in or life gets loud, come back to what's written here. Re-read your notes, re-center your beliefs, and remind yourself who's in charge.

Every belief in this appendix is a seed, and the way you tend to it determines what grows next. Water it with consistency, patience, and purpose. Pull the weeds of doubt when they appear. And when the storms come, remember: deep roots don't fear the wind.

You are the Chief Investment Officer of your life. Lead accordingly. Keep planting. Keep leading. Keep growing.

The harvest is coming.

I NEED A FAVOR...

If this book helped you see money differently, I'd be truly grateful if you took a minute to leave a short review on Amazon, Goodreads, or wherever you bought it. Your words mean more than you think. They might be exactly what someone else needs to hear, helping someone who's still searching for hope and clarity find the message they've been missing. Your review also helps me continue my mission of "providing the financial education schools didn't."

STACKERS UNIVERSITY

CONTINUE YOUR TRANSFORMATION AT STACKERSUNIVERSITY.COM

NOT SURE WHAT TO WRITE? JUST SHARE WHAT PART OF THE BOOK SPOKE TO YOU MOST OR HOW IT HELPED YOU SEE MONEY DIFFERENTLY.

Amazon.com   Stackersuniversity.com   Goodreads.com

DEDICATION

This guide is dedicated to three people who represent my "why," the real reason this project exists.

To my "little sister," Tea –
Thank you for being brave enough to say, "I want to invest, but I don't know where to start." You asked a question so many people are too ashamed to admit. Your honesty inspired the foundation of this entire guide. I wanted to give you more than an answer; I wanted to build you a blueprint. This is for you, and for every person who has the heart to start but needs the right guide to begin.

To my Son –
You just turned 22, and you're standing at the beginning of a road I wish someone had mapped out for me. This is everything I wish I knew when I was your age – not just the tactics, but the truth. The mindset, the game, and the mission. I built this so you could run farther, faster, and freer than I ever did. May this be the start of a legacy that changes everything, not just for you, but for those who come after you.

And to my Daughter –
You're only 11 now, but one day you'll read this and understand. This world – especially when it comes to money – doesn't teach girls to lead. It doesn't teach women to build wealth, only how to clip coupons, "shop smart," and justify spending with gimmicks like "girl math." I reject that. I reject that for you. Girl math won't fund your freedom. You don't need better tricks. You need power, ownership, and a wealth cycle of your own. You are not here to play small. You are not here to be at anyone's mercy. You are the author of your own story, and I wrote this so money will never be the reason you say "no" to your dreams.

The Ultimate Dedication

Everything I do is dedicated to the one person who represents the "why" behind Dr. Stacker and Stackers University:

To my wife, Mrs. Stacker -
Without you, there would be no Dr. Stacker and no Stackers University. Thank you for making the sacrifices that gave me the time and space to pursue my passions, to explore this crazy idea of a YouTube Channel and then a book. **Your sacrifices have not gone unnoticed, they've been the quiet strength behind every word, every idea, every video, every book, and every breakthrough.**

Many years ago, you came into my life and saved me. More than being my partner, you became my biggest *why* - the reason I was able to change my life. Because of you, I've become a better version of myself every day: a better father, a better husband, a better friend, and a better man.

I can't thank you enough, and I can't fully express how much I love you.

ROOTED IN LOVE
GROWING IN PURPOSE
02/22/24

ABOUT THE AUTHOR

Dr. Stacker, also known as Doc Stacker, Ph.D., was introduced to the world in March 2022 with the launch of Stackers University and its YouTube channel. His mission is clear: to create content dedicated to "providing the financial education the school system did NOT provide." Doc teaches like your favorite professor, challenges you like a coach, speaks to you like a counselor, and keeps it real like your wise uncle as he helps people break free from the "Working Poor Cycle" and build wealth on purpose.

Doc teaches like your favorite professor, challenges you like a coach, speaks to you like a counselor, and keeps it real like your wise uncle - helping people break free from the Working Poor Cycle and build wealth on purpose.

Doc didn't start wealthy. His financial journey began with just $5,000, and through hustle, discipline, and vision, he grew that seed into a multi-million-dollar real estate portfolio. On the outside, it looked like he had "made it." But his financial house was built on sand. When the pressure hit, it all collapsed. He lost the portfolio, went deep into debt, and found himself trapped in the same cycle where even six-figure earners live paycheck to paycheck, broke, and enslaved by debt.

That collapse became the turning point. Out of failure, he rebuilt by cracking the code, discovering that wealth isn't just about what you do, but who you become. As he says, "It's not easy, but it is simple." By transforming his mindset, mastering his emotions, and aligning his identity with his financial goals, he created the Stackers University Wealth Cycle™, a system born from failure that helped him save $250,000 in just three years.

As an educator with nearly three decades in higher education as a professor and administrator, Doc Stacker brings together the rigor of academia, the insights of behavioral finance, the grit of lived experience, and the wisdom of someone who has walked the same hard road to wealth. With a Master's in Counseling and a Ph.D. in Educational Leadership, he integrates psychology, emotion, and practical investing into a framework that changes lives.

Today, Doc teaches people how to break free from the Working Poor Cycle by focusing less on "tips and tricks" and more on identity transformation. Most financial advice gets stuck on surface-level hacks: budget harder, cut back, maybe even skip your daily latte as if that alone builds generational wealth. Doc knows the truth firsthand: the barrier isn't knowing what to do, the barrier is becoming the kind of person who can actually do it. Once that shift happens, the actions take care of themselves.

His teaching blends personal finance, investing, and behavioral psychology into a practical playbook for anyone tired of surviving and ready to thrive. At the heart of his work is a conviction: the most valuable real estate in the world is the space between your two ears. When you lead like a CIO, plant like a gardener, and align your mindset with your money, you build wealth that lasts.

The journey doesn't end here. Keep learning with Doc and the Stackers University community.

Website: https://www.stackersuniversity.com

YouTube: Stackers University

Chapter Forty-Five

YOUR NOTA BENE NOTES

Use This Space To Collect Ideas You Want To "Note Well" For Yourself

www.ingramcontent.com/pod-product-compliance
Lightning Source LLC
Chambersburg PA
CBHW021105130626
46554CB00002B/546